TO THE MOON!

The Honeymooners®

book of Trivia

John Katsigeorgis

FRIEDMAN/FAIRFAX

A FRIEDMAN/FAIRFAX BOOK
©2002 by Michael Friedman Publishing Group, Inc.

Library of Congress Cataloging-in-Publication Data available upon request.

ISBN 1-58663-787-8

Editor: Nathaniel Marunas
Art Director: Kevin Ullrich
Designer: Kevin Baier
Photography Editor: Janice Ackerman
Production Manager: Richela Fabian Morgan

Color separations by Radstock Repro
Printed in England by Butler & Tanner Ltd

1 3 5 7 9 10 8 6 4 2

To my beautiful wife, Eva, whose dedication and long hours of watching *The Honeymooners* with me were essential in turning this hare-brained scheme into reality. Baby, you're the greatest!

I would like to thank the following people for all the invaluable help they provided in completing this project: Craig Horwich, who painstakingly assembled what is the most complete listing of *Honeymooners* episodes that has yet made it into print; Ben Okuley, who helped me compile air dates and other crucial facts about many of the episodes, especially those from the 1960s; and the staff at the Friedman/Fairfax Publishing Group, including editor Nathaniel Marunas, art director Kevin Ullrich, designer Kevin Baier, photo researchers Kathleen Wolfe and Janice Ackerman, and production wizard Richela Morgan.

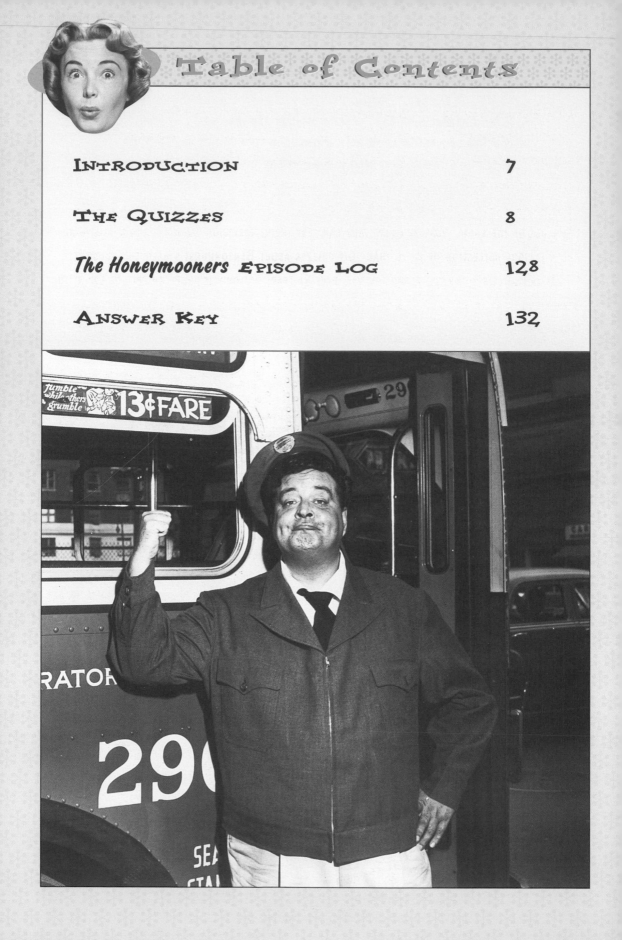

Table of Contents

Introduction

JACKIE GLEASON'S BELOVED EVERYMAN CHARACTER FROM *CAVALCADE OF STARS*, LOUDMOUTH BUS DRIVER RALPH KRAMDEN, WAS THE SEED FROM WHICH ONE OF THE MOST ENDURING TELEVISION SITCOMS OF ALL TIME WOULD GROW. *THE HONEYMOONERS*, WHICH STARTED AS A SKETCH ON *CAVALCADE*, GREW TO BECOME ONE OF THE MOST POPULAR—AND IS TODAY ONE OF THE MOST SYNDICATED—SHOWS EVER BROADCAST ON TV. NOW, IN CELEBRATION OF THE FIFTIETH ANNIVERSARY OF THE BIRTH OF THE SHOW, *HONEYMOONERS* FANS CAN TEST THEIR TELEVISION IQ WITH THIS CHALLENGING AND HILARIOUS COLLECTION OF MORE THAN 100 QUIZZES ABOUT BENSONHURST'S BELOVED FOURSOME.

IF THE QUIZZES STUMP YOU ALONG THE WAY, HAVE NO FEAR: NOT ONLY IS THERE AN EPISODE LOG AT THE BACK OF THE BOOK THAT IS MORE COMPLETE THAN ANYTHING EVER PUBLISHED BEFORE, THE ANSWER KEY APPEARS RIGHT BEHIND IT. FOR YOUR CONVENIENCE EACH ANSWER IS MARKED, WHERE APPROPRIATE, WITH THE EPISODE NUMBER WHERE THE ANSWER CAN BE FOUND. SO SHARPEN YOUR PENCILS, PUT ON YOUR THINKING CAPS, AND GET READY FOR A FUN-FILLED RAMBLE DOWN THE STREETS OF *HONEYMOONERS*-ERA BENSONHURST.

Episode Warm-up

HERE'S A LITTLE QUIZ TO HELP YOU WARM UP THE OL' SOUP BONE. SEE IF YOU CAN MATCH THE EPISODE THEMES LISTED ON THE LEFT WITH THE TITLE OF THE EPISODE IN WHICH THEY OCCURRED ON THE RIGHT.

1. Ralph and Ed manage a boxer.

2. Ralph is in a Choosy Chews commercial.

3. The Kramdens buy a two-family house in Flushing, Queens.

4. The bus company psychiatrist tells Ralph to stay away from Ed Norton.

5. Ralph thinks Alice is being unfaithful with his best friend.

6. Alice thinks Ralph is being unfaithful.

7. Ralph breaks his leg in a bus accident.

8. Ralph thinks he's been fired, but he's actually been promoted to traffic manager.

9. Ralph thinks Alice is trying to kill him.

10. Ralph takes Ed to the movies for his birthday, and Ed wins a television set.

A. "The Little Man Who Wasn't There"

B. "A Matter of Record"

C. "The Brother-in-Law"

D. "Cupid"

E. "Finders Keepers"

F. "Kramden vs. Norton"

G. "The Lawsuit"

H. "Letter to the Boss"

I. "The Love Letter"

J. "Mind Your Own Business"

11. Ralph and Ed get another job to make some extra money, because Ralph thinks he is going to be a father.

12. Ralph and Ed buy a hotel in New Jersey.

13. Ralph and Ed want to buy a neighborhood candy store.

14. The Kramdens and Nortons enter a Racoon Lodge costume contest.

15. Ralph insults Alice's mother, and Alice leaves Ralph.

16. Ralph is named in a millionaire's will.

17. The Kramdens and Nortons go dancing and roller-skating.

18. Ralph tries to land a better job by taking a civil service exam.

19. Ralph's boss offers Norton an executive position at the bus company.

20. Ed tries his luck at selling irons after getting fired from his job in the sewer.

Theme Song Stumper

THE MUSIC TO *The Honeymooners* THEME SONG RINGS WITH FAMILIARITY, BUT THE LYRICS WERE NEVER SUNG. SEE HOW MUCH YOU REALLY KNOW ABOUT THE SHOW'S OPENER.

1. See if you can complete the song's lyrics by filling in the blanks.

   "You're my greatest love. You're _____, you're stars from _____."

   "You set my _____ afire with _____ constantly."

   "You're my _____ dream. To hold you close is my greatest _____."

   "The vision of your _____ in my arms haunting ____."

   "I can't _____ the words that all the _____ seem to reveal."

   "Simple words like _____ and soul hold the _____ that I feel."

   "You're my _____ love. For _____ there will be no _____ love."

   "So give your _____ to me, let this be our greatest _____."

2. Who wrote the lyrics to *The Honeymooners* theme song?
   A. Jackie Gleason
   B. Bill Templeton
   C. Ray Bloch
   D. Duke Enston

3. Who is credited with writing the music to the song?
   A. Jackie Gleason
   B. Bill Templeton
   C. Ray Bloch
   D. Duke Enston

4. Which record company published the song? (Hint: It's the same publishing company that Ralph and Ed tried to sell their song to in "Songwriters.")

Just This Once

Each of these characters appeared in only one *Honeymooners* episode. Can you put a name to the face? As an added challenge, see if you can name the episode in which they appeared.

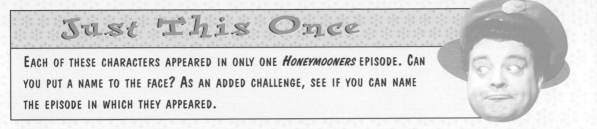

1. H_____ L____ B_____

2. D_____ M____

3. Mr. _____

4. Dr. _____

5. Nurse _____

6. C_____ S_____

7. H_____ G_____

8. T____ M_____

9. A_____ P_____

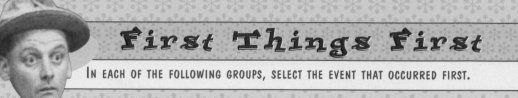

First Things First

1. A. Ralph finds a baby on the bus.
B. Ralph finds a suitcase on the bus.
C. Joe Cassidy finds $1,000.00 on the bus.

2. A. Ed plays a harmonica.
B. Ed plays a coronet.
C. Ed plays a piano.

3. A. Ralph dances the Hucklebuck.
B. Ralph dances with Joe Malone's fiancée.
C. Ralph dances with Harriett Muller.

4. A. Ed dances with Frances Langford.
B. Ed dances with Harriett Muller.
C. Ed dances with a bowl of plaster.

5. A. The Kramdens are on a quiz show sponsored by a bread company.
B. The Kramdens are on *Beat the Clock*.
C. Ralph is on *The $99,000 Answer*.

6. A. Ralph breaks his leg in a bus accident.
B. Ralph hurts his back while bowling.
C. Ralph has a toothache.

7. A. Alice's sister Agnes gets married.
B. Alice's sister Sally gets married.
C. Alice's aunt Ethel gets married.

8. A. Ed is wearing Trixie's dress.
B. Ed is dressed as Clara Bow.
C. Ed is dressed as Pierre Françoise de la Brioski.

9. A. Rudy the Repairman stops by the Kramden apartment.
B. Joe the Bartender stops by the Kramden apartment.
C. Fenwick Babbitt stops by the Kramden apartment.

10. A. Ralph Kramden meets Art Carney.
B. Ed Norton meets Jackie Gleason.
C. Ralph and Ed see Audrey Meadows.

11. A. Ralph and Ed buy a hotel.
B. Ralph and Ed buy a hot dog stand.
C. Ralph and Ed buy a summer cottage.

12. A. Ralph buys an iron.
B. Ralph buys a vacuum cleaner.
C. Ralph buys a two-family house.

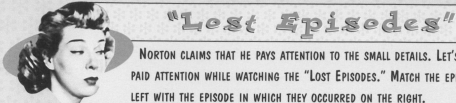

"Lost Episodes" ID

Norton claims that he pays attention to the small details. Let's see how well you paid attention while watching the "Lost Episodes." Match the episode details on the left with the episode in which they occurred on the right.

1. Alice burns Ralph's feet with hot water.

2. Ralph gets his hand stuck in a candy jar.

3. Norton hits Ralph on the knee with a hammer.

4. Ralph lies down on a cot and it collapses.

5. Ed spills the beans about Trixie really being a brunette, not a blonde.

6. Ed carries Trixie out of the Kramden apartment.

7. The Kramdens borrow the Nortons' furniture.

8. Ralph is wearing a Brooklyn Dodgers cap.

9. Ed is wearing a pair of yellow shoes that he won in a mambo contest.

10. There's a birthday party going on in the sewer for Alphonse.

11. Ed tells us the story of when he got hit on the head with a ball at a baseball game at Ebbets Field.

12. Ed puts a box full of empty liquor bottles on the Kramdens' table.

13. Ed is carrying his laundry in a paper bag.

14. The cleaners tell Alice that the stain on Ralph's lodge uniform is beer.

15. Alice is washing the outside of the kitchen window.

A. "The Little Man Who Wasn't There"

B. "The Brother-in-Law"

C. "Expectant Fathers"

D. "Game Called on Account of Marriage"

E. "Guest Speaker"

F. "Hair-Raising Tale"

G. "The Lawsuit"

H. "Lucky Number"

I. "Manager of the Baseball Team"

J. "Move Uptown"

K. "Norton Moves In"

L. "Ralph's Sweet Tooth"

M. "Songs and Witty Sayings"

N. "Stars over Flatbush"

O. "Teamwork Beat the Clock"

16. Alice is in the driver's seat of a car.

17. Ralph installs three extra locks on his door to keep Norton out.

18. Ralph accidentally fires a handgun in his apartment.

19. Alice purposely breaks a plate on the kitchen floor.

20. Ralph tries to kill a mouse with a broom.

P. "The Adoption"

Q. "The Cold"

R. "The Great Jewel Robbery"

S. "The Prowler"

T. "Vacation at Fred's Landing"

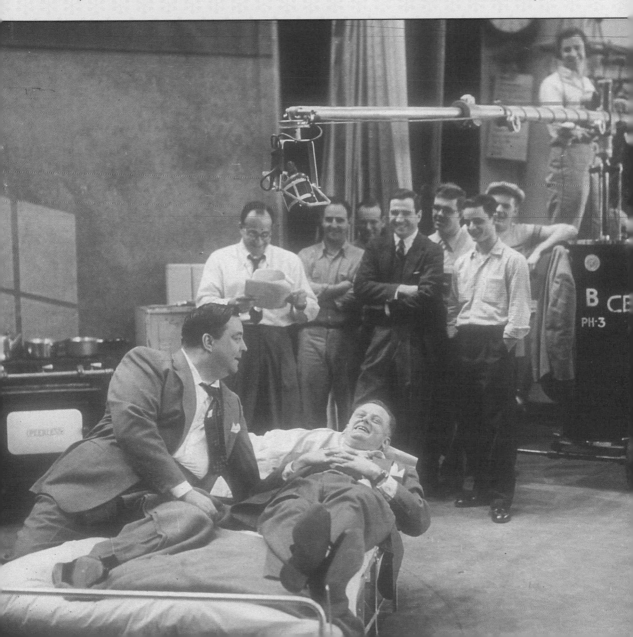

Don't I Know You?

RALPH KRAMDEN ISN'T THE ONLY CHARACTER PLAYED BY JACKIE GLEASON ON *THE HONEYMOONERS*. CAN YOU IDENTIFY THE FOLLOWING SIX CHARACTERS WHO ALSO MADE THEIR WAY ON TO THE SHOW?

1. _____

2. _____

3. _____

4. _____

5. _____

6. _____

Korpulant Kramden

THROUGH THE YEARS, RALPH WAS TEASED FOR BEING "A LITTLE OVERWEIGHT." SEE HOW WELL YOU REMEMBER THESE WEIGHTY WISECRACKS BY FILLING IN THE BLANKS

1. "Some kids are _____, some kids are _____, fatso Kramden is the only kid who walks down the _____ _____ to _____."
—Bill Davis wrote this in Ralph's yearbook.

2. Ralph (referring to a measly $600.00): "Peanuts! Peanuts! What am I gonna do with peanuts?"
    Alice: "Eat 'em. Like _____ _____ _____."

3. Ralph: "I'm not the type of person that eats and runs."
    Alice: "Eats and runs? With the way you eat, you're _____ _____ _____ _____ _____."

4. Ralph: "There isn't anything in this world that will stop me from going down in the sewer tomorrow."
Alice: "Oh no? There isn't a _____ in this _____ that you can _____ _____."

5. "Boy oh boy. How could anyone so _____ be so _____?"
—Ed Norton, after hearing Ralph's hip lingo.

6. Ralph: "At last I have a bathtub that I can be comfortable in."
    Alice: "What did you order, a _____ _____?"

7. Ralph: "I need some money, and I know that you have it somewhere around here, and you will let me have it, ol' wonderful doll."
    Alice: "Oh no I won't, you adorable _____ _____ _____."

8. Ralph: "It won't hurt me to wait a couple of hours to eat."
    Ed: "It won't hurt you, but it'll be _____ on the _____."

9. "If they pay by the _____, Alice will be a _____."
—Ed Norton, when Ralph considers selling his body to science.

10. "You didn't have to go to work without your bath. You could have stopped by the _____. They wouldn't mind _____ one more _____."
—Trixie, to Ralph after he complained that Ed took too long in the bathroom.

Family Matters

You know that I know that you know everything about the Kramdens and the Nortons. But how well do you know their extended families?

1. What is Ralph's mother's full maiden name?

2. How many siblings does Ralph have?
   A. none   B. 4
   C. 7   D. 12

3. What is Alice's father's first name?
   A. Mike   B. George
   C. Leo   D. Fred

4. How many siblings does Alice have?
   A. none   B. 4
   C. 7   D. 12

5. What is Ed Norton's mother's maiden name?

6. How many siblings does Ed have?
   A. none   B. 4
   C. 7   D. 12

7. How many siblings does Trixie have?
   A. none   B. 4
   C. 7   D. 12

8. Where does Trixie's mother live?

9. Who has an uncle who was hit by a pickle truck?
   A. Alice   B. Ed
   C. Ralph   D. Trixie

10. Match each of Alice's relatives with his or her place of residence:
    A. Her grandmother   Astoria
    B. Her mother   Buffalo
    C. Uncle George   Dayton
    D. Aunt Edna   Galway, Ireland
    E. Aunt Ethel Delaney   Pittsburgh

Facts and Figures

THEY SAY THE DEVIL IS IN THE DETAILS, BUT DON'T LET THESE TIDBITS GET YOU HOT UNDER THE COLLAR.

1. How many episodes of *The Honeymooners* are currently in syndication or readily available on video?
A. 39 C. 124
B. 116 D. 173

2. Which network broadcast *The Honeymooners* as a stand-alone show for a single season?
A. DuMont C. CBS
B. ABC D. NBC

3. The Honeymooners originated as a short skit on which of the following shows?
A. *American Scene Magazine*
B. *Cavalcade of Stars*
C. *The Jackie Gleason Show*
D. *You're in the Picture*

4. On what night of the week was *The Jackie Gleason Show* broadcast?
A. Saturday C. Tuesday
B. Sunday D. Friday

5. Who was Jackie Gleason's primary orchestra leader in the 1950s?

6. Who was Jackie Gleason's primary orchestra leader on his 1960s variety show?

7. In 1954, while Gleason was out of action with a broken leg, Art Carney did a parody in which he played Ed Norton's father. What was this parody called?

8. Which of the following was NOT an original sponsor of *The Jackie Gleason Show*?
A. Schick
B. Schaeffer Snorkel Pens
C. Nestlé Instant Coffee
D. Ford Motor Company

9. Who was Jackie Gleason's manager?
A. Killer Cuoco C. Bullets Durgom
B. Knuckles Grogan D. Chester Barnes

10. Who was NOT married to Jackie Gleason?
A. Linda Miller C. Beverly McKittrick
B. Marilyn Taylor D. Genevieve Halford

11. What was the shortest-running *Honeymooners* sketch from the 1950s?

12. What was the longest-running *Honeymooners* sketch from the 1950s?

1. _____

2. _____

3. _____

4. _____

5. _____

6. _____

7. _____

8. _____

9. _____

Q & A

WHEN YOU ASK A QUESTION OF A HONEYMOONER, YOU CAN ALWAYS EXPECT SOME SORT OF SMART-ALECK ANSWER. SEE IF YOU REMEMBER THE REPLIES TO THE FOLLOWING QUESTIONS.

1. Ed (lying in a bunk above Ralph): "Hey Ralph, mind if I smoke?"
Ralph: "_____."

2. Ed (trying to find out what's wrong with the toaster): "The radiostat conductor is not making proper contact with the electro coil."
Alice: "What does that mean?"
Ed: "_____."

3. Trixie (after hearing Ed tell Ralph that he sold many irons): "Ed, did your first day on the job really go well?"
Ed: "_____."

4. Ralph (after sparying some perfume in the room): "Well, how do you like the perfume?"
Ed: "_____."

5. Ralph (referring to a Racoon Lodge member): "Do you know what it's like to be a thirteen-tail man?"
Alice: "It must be pretty special, since _____."

6. Ralph: "The bills will get bigger and bigger, and I'll get less to eat. Then you know what I'll look like?"
Alice: "Yeah, a _____."

7. Ralph (after finding out that Norton is getting a ride to work): "Can I get a lift?"
Ed: "Sure, there's always room _____."

8. Ralph (after Alice tells him that she didn't get a chance to sew his socks): "What could be a bigger job than sewing my socks?"
Alice: "I was _____."

9. Ed is buying some new furniture, and the store sends Ralph a letter of reference to fill out.
Letter: "How long have you known the applicant?"
Ralph: "_____."
Letter: "Do you consider the applicant trustworthy?"
Ralph: "_____."
Letter: "In your opinion, is the applicant of good character?"
Ralph: "The applicant _____."

10. Ralph (his finger is sticking through a hole in his shoe): "What's going to happen if I walk around like this all night?"
Alice: "_____."

Who Said That?

1. _____: "Someday you're going to ask me to do something for you."
   _____: "I'm asking you right now. Leave the premises."

2. _____: "Excuse me, honey."
   _____: "Who are you calling 'honey'?"
   _____: "Norton, who else?"

3. _____: "You're making a very big mistake."
   _____: "Yeah. We're big shots."

4. _____ (referring to his mother-in-law): "If she ever got on that *$64,000 Question*, her category would be 'Nasty.'"
   _____: "Well, if she ever got to the last question, she'd have to bring my mother-in-law along as an expert."

5. _____: "Taste this appetizer and tell me what you think of it."
   _____: "This stuff is great. It's very good."
   _____: "Hey, this is dog food!"

6. _____: "I promised my friend Ralph Kramden that I'd start the show off with a bang."

7. _____: "Don't say 'Okay.' From now on say 'Very good, sir.'"
   _____: "Okay."

8. _____: "I've got no compunction about doing this, Ralph. You know why? Because I'm a bum, bum, bum..."

9. _____: "What's the matter, man? Aren't ya hip? Don't ya dig?"

10. _____: "Did you notice when he came in how his voice filled this room?"
    _____: "I did notice that the room got a little crowded."

Out of Place

1. "Pickles"
   "Expectant Fathers"
   "The Adoption"
   "Santa Claus and the Bookies"

2. Grace Kelly's father
   Oscar of the Waldorf
   Pierre of the Ritz
   Andre of the Plaza

3. "Vacation at Fred's Landing"
   "Manager of the Baseball Team"
   "What's Her Name Again?"
   "The Lawsuit"

4. Stanley Diamond
   Bill Davis
   Chester Barnes
   Fred Beatty

5. Darven
   Blitzen
   Prancer
   Dancer

6. *The Complete Works of William Shakespeare*
   David Copperfield
   Tom Sawyer
   A Tale of Two Cities

7. Chartreuse
   Violet
   Red
   Midnight black

8. Eggplant purple
   Robin's egg blue
   Strawberry red
   Canary yellow

9. Little Jack Little
   Isham Jones
   Ted Fiorito
   Basil Fomeen

10. Tommy Manicotti
    Johnny Bennett
    Fogarty boy
    Garrity boy

11. "Mama Loves Mambo"
    "Dial J for Janitor"
    "The Bensonhurst Bomber"
    "The Worry Wart"

12. Freddy Muller
    Mr. Wilson
    Bibbo
    Dick Prescott

Mug Shots

PICTURED HERE ARE BENSONHURST'S ELEVEN MOST WANTED CRIMINALS. MATCH EACH PICTURE WITH THE CROOKS' NAMES AND THE CRIMES THEY COMMITTED.

NAME

MARTY

BOSS AND ZIGGY

JOE

BARNEY HACKETT

GUS STEINHART

ROCKY AND LEFTY

BULLETS DURGOM

DANNY AND BIBBO

WANTED FOR

ARMED ROBBERY

BOOKMAKING

COUNTERFEITING

FRAUD

MURDER/BANK ROBBERY

MURDER/JAILBREAK

RACKETEERING

RACKETEERING (BOSS)

1. _____ _____

2. _____ _____

3. _____ _____

4. _____ _____

5. _____ _____

6. _____ _____

7. _____ _____

8. _____ _____

25

Bensonhurst's Most Wanted

THE KRAMDENS AND NORTONS RAN INTO THEIR SHARE OF TROUBLE WITH THE CRIMINAL ELEMENT. LET'S SEE HOW MUCH YOU REMEMBER ABOUT THESE TV VILLAINS.

1. In "Guest Speaker," a prowler climbs in through the Kramdens' window and hits Ralph on the head with something. What was the weapon?
   A. a gun
   B. a wooden club
   C. a rubber whip
   D. a bottle

2. In "The Finger Man," Ralph helps catch a wanted murderer. At what street does the thug board Ralph's bus?
   A. 42nd Street
   B. 48th Street
   C. 62nd Street
   D. 68th Street

3. In "Santa Claus and the Bookies," where do the bookmakers hold interviews for a street Santa?
   A. on the corner of 8th and Montgomery streets
   B. in a run-down warehouse
   C. in an office building on Park Avenue
   D. in a hotel room

4. In "Santa Claus and the Bookies," the bookies use aliases when introducing themselves to Ralph. What does Ralph think their names are?
   A. Mr. Simon and Mr. Smith
   B. Mr. Smith and Mr. Smith
   C. Mr. Bibbo and Boss
   D. Mr. Lefty and Mr. Rocky

5. In "Hair-Raising Tale," a bald guy wearing a wig swindles Ralph and Ed. What is the swindler's name?
   A. Gus Steinhart
   B. Bullets Durgom
   C. Chester Barnes
   D. Knuckles Grogan

6. In "The Great Jewel Robbery," Ed calls a coworker (who is an amateur actor) and asks him to stage a robbery at Ralph's apartment. What is the man's name?
   A. Bruce Hupfelt
   B. Joe Cassidy
   C. Henry Becke
   D. Frank Brady

7. In "The Great Jewel Robbery," a real thief shows up at the Kramden apartment before the actor gets there. What is the crook's name?
   A. Joe
   B. Jim
   C. Bibbo
   D. Ziggy

8. In "Funny Money," Ralph mistakes the counterfeiters for cops, but they don't put one over on Norton, who says they're what?
   A. criminals
   B. from a law firm
   C. from an insurance company
   D. from an investment firm

9. In "Stand In for Murder," Jackie Gleason plays a mob boss who looks like Ralph. What is the boss's name?
   A. Nick
   B. Harry
   C. Marty
   D. Charlie

10. In "Stand In for Murder," the mob tries to set up Ralph to get bumped off by which rival gang leader?
    A. Barney Hackett
    B. Knuckles Grogan
    C. Bullets Durgom
    D. Killer Cuoco

Complete the Quote

1. "You've come to me before with a chance to make a _____. I can't stand to make a _____ again. I'm _____ _____."
—Ed Norton, after Ralph offers to let him in on another moneymaking venture.

2. "Leave it there, the _____ will get it."
—Ed Norton, after a cookie falls on the floor.

3. "Yawning? That sounded like _____ time at the _____."
—Alice, referring to a loud obnoxious sound made by a suffering Ralph, who says it was a yawn.

4. "Don't touch me, Ralph, I'm _____."
—Ed Norton, after Ralph asks him to impersonate a doctor.

5. "Since I met you, my sewer has become a _____ ___ _____."
—Ed Norton, in a letter he once wrote to Trixie.

6. "I can't help it, Ralph. I'm a sick man. I'm a _____."
—Ed Norton, after getting caught looking in the Kramden icebox.

7. "Before I see you go to work, I'd rather see you _____."
—Ralph, after Alice offers to get a job because Ralph thinks he's been fired.

8. "The _____ sprocket is causing interference, which in turn causes the _____ line to interfere with the _____ in the Dynaflow."
—Ed Norton, after looking over Ralph's broken vacuum cleaner.

9. "When I leave [work] to come home expecting a decent meal, what happens? A neighbor tells me that she saw you begging the _____ _____ for my _____."
—Ralph, during an argument with Alice.

10. "Official _____ helmet off, _____ _____, wherever you are."
—Ed Norton, watching TV in the Kramden apartment.

27

First Honeymoon

HERE ARE A DOZEN QUESTIONS TO TEST JUST HOW WELL ACQUAINTED YOU ARE WITH SOME IMPORTANT HONEYMOONERS FIRSTS.

1. The very first Honeymooners skit was telecast on which network?
   A. ABC
   B. CBS
   C. NBC
   D. DuMont

2. On what date did Americans get their first-ever glimpse of *The Honeymooners*?
   A. February 17, 1951
   B. October 5, 1951
   C. January 26, 1952
   D. September 27, 1952

3. In "Forgot to Register," what is the first name of the candidate who Ralph and Ed are campaigning for?
   A. Jack
   B. Phil
   C. Walter
   D. Harvey

4. Ralph thinks he won first prize in the Teresa Grotta raffle, but he really won 26th prize. What was first prize?

5. In which episode do we see the jacket of a Racoon uniform for the first time?

6. What was the first Honeymooners episode to run more than thirty minutes?

7. The Kramdens and Nortons end up in court over a TV set. Who was the first witness called to the stand?
   A. Ralph
   C. Ed
   B. Alice
   D. Trixie

8. Ralph is spending counterfeit money all over town. Who does he give his first phony $100.00 bill to?
   A. a police officer
   B. a telephone repairman
   C. Alice's mother
   D. Tommy Doyle

9. What was the first Honeymooners episode filmed with intention for syndication?

10. Ralph is collecting money to buy the boss's daughter a wedding present. Who is the first bus driver we see him get $2.00 from?
    A. Muller
    B. Cassidy
    C. Gallagher
    D. Reilly

11. In "Unconventional Behavior," what is the first item Ralph takes out of his bag of gags to show to Norton?

12. According to Mrs. Manicotti in "A Weighty Problem," what is Mr. Manicotti's first name?

At the Movies

ALICE AND TRIXIE ALWAYS COMPLAINED THAT RALPH AND ED NEVER TOOK THEM OUT—I GUESS THE GIRLS DIDN'T CONSIDER GOING TO THE MOVIES A NIGHT OUT. PROVE YOURSELF A MOVIE BUFF BY ANSWERING ALL THESE QUESTIONS CORRECTLY.

1. Match the event on the left with the episode in which it occurred on the right.

A. The Kramdens and Nortons go to a movie at the Loews Twilight Theater down the street.

"Double Anniversary"

B. The Nortons are going to a movie at the Loews Pitkin Theater.

"Champagne and Caviar"

C. Alice invites Trixie to go see a German film at a foreign movie house.

"Letter to the Boss"

D. Ralph begs Alice to go to the movies with him.

"The Love Letter"

E. Ralph treats Alice and the Nortons to a movie for Ed's birthday.

"The Babysitter"

F. Ralph thinks Alice lied about going to the movies last Wednesday.

"What's Her Name Again?"

G. Alice blatantly lies to Ralph about going to the movies to see a love story.

"Kramden vs. Norton"

2. Referring to question 1A, which movie do the Kramdens see?

3. Referring to question 1A, who of the following is NOT in the movie?
A. Ronald Coleman   C. Lana Turner
B. Ronald Reagan   D. Millicent Brady

4. Referring to question 1B, why don't the Kramdens join the Nortons?

5. Referring to question 1D, what movie does Ralph tell Alice he wants to see?

6. Referring to question 1E, what movie theater do they go to, and what other movie is playing there besides *The Desert Hawk*?

7. Referring to question 1E, who of the following is NOT in the cast of *The Desert Hawk*?
A. Richard Greene   C. Jackie Gleason
B. Ray Bloch   D. Yvonne De Carlo

8. Referring to question 1F, who does Ralph think Alice was with on Wednesday?

9. Referring to question 1G, where is Alice really going?

10. What is the name of the theater that holds an annual amateur night?

Who's Who

SEE HOW MUCH YOU REALLY KNOW ABOUT THE PEOPLE WHO PLAYED OUR FAVORITE HONEYMOONERS.

1. True or False: Art Carney's first character on The Honeymooners was Ed Norton.

2. How many actresses have played the role of Alice Kramden?

3. Name all the actresses from question **2** in order from first to last.

4. How many actresses have played the role of Trixie Norton?

5. Name all the actresses from question 4 in order from first to last.

6. Which actor/actress played one of the four main characters, was born in China, and learned to speak English as a second language?

7. What is Jackie Gleason's birth name?

8. What is Art Carney's birth name?

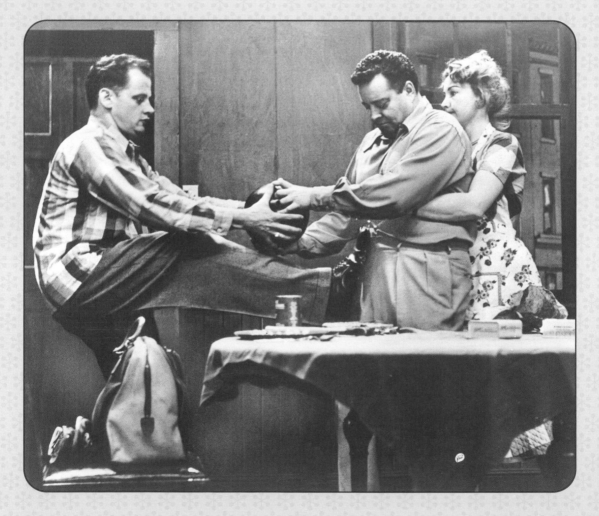

Money Matters

RALPH AND ALICE HAVE DIFFERENT IDEAS ABOUT HOW TO SPEND RALPH'S INCOME.
HERE'S AN OPPORTUNITY TO SEE WHOSE SIDE OF THE COIN YOU'RE ON.

1. Ralph and Alice hold the record for the all-time lowest gas bill. How much was it?

2. Ralph lost the money that the Racoon Lodge collected for their annual dance. How much was it?

3. How much did Ralph and Ed pay for the 2,000 Handy Housewife Helper tools?
   A) $200.00   C) $500.00
   B) $400.00   D) $1000.00

4. In "Please Leave the Premises," the landlord raises the Kramdens' rent. How much did they pay before the increase?
   A) $33.33   C) $41.12
   B) $36.58   D) $44.44

5. In "A Woman's Work Is Never Done," Ralph gets Norton to help him with the housework. How much does Norton charge him?
   A) 25 cents/hour   C) $1.00/hour
   B) 50 cents/hour   D) $1.50/hour

6. How much money do Ralph and Alice have in war bonds?
   A) $4.68   C) $62.00
   B) $12.83   D) $168.32

7. What is first prize at the Racoons' annual costume party?
   A) $5.00   C) $50.00
   B) $10.00   D) $100.00

8. How much do Ralph and Ed pay for the hot dog stand in New Jersey?

9. In "Boxtop Kid," how much does Ralph spend on products in his effort to win a contest?
   A) $7.50   C) $23.50
   B) $12.50   D) $32.50

10. How much does Alice get paid to baby-sit Harvey Wahlstetter Jr.?
   A) 25 cents/hour   C) 75 cents/hour
   B) 50 cents/hour   D) $1.00/hour

Police Blotter

RALPH WAS CERTAINLY NO STRANGER TO LOCAL LAW ENFORCEMENT PERSONNEL. WHEN HE WASN'T HELPING TO CATCH CRIMINALS, HE WAS BUSY GETTING HIMSELF AND ED INTO SOME SORT OF TROUBLE WITH THE LAW. HERE ARE TEN QUESTIONS DEVOTED TO RALPH'S INTERACTIONS WITH THE MEN IN BLUE.

1. In "Letter to the Boss," Ralph and Ed are plotting to remove a letter from a mailbox, when a policeman overhears them. Where are they at the time?

A. in the bowling alley's locker room
B. outside the bowling alley
C. outside their apartment building
D. in the park

2. In "The Finger Man," the police chief goes to the Kramden apartment to congratulate Ralph. What is his name?

A. Casey   C. Brady
B. Kelly   D. Riley

3. In "The Finger Man," two police officers hide in the Kramdens' bedroom to try to catch Bullets Durgom. What are their names?

A. Maloney and Casey
B. Brady and Kelly
C. Maloney and Brady
D. Casey and Kelly

4. In "Move Uptown," a police officer thinks Ralph is robbing an apartment. How does Ralph ultimately prove his innocence?

A. He wakes up the building's superintendent.
B. He shows his driver's license.
C. He asks Ed to explain.
D. He shows his lease.

5. In "Funny Money," a police officer is going door to door collecting money. What is the money for?

A. the annual Policeman's Ball
B. a children's party at the youth center
C. to help feed the hungry and homeless abroad
D. to help build a recreation area in the neighborhood

6. In "Stand In for Murder," a police officer walks into a bar and saves Ralph's life. How?

A. He tells Ralph to move his car.
B. He arrests the crooks who were going to kill Ralph.
C. He sits down to have a drink with Ralph.
D. He hears a noise and goes in to investigate.

7. In "The Great Jewel Robbery," Officer Callahan stops by the Kramden residence to sell tickets to the Policeman's Ball. How many tickets does Alice buy, and how much does each one cost?

A. one/$5.00   C. two/$1.50

B. one/$3.00   D. two/$3.00

8. Some neighbors ask Ralph to place bets for them when he goes to the track. The police suspect that Ralph is a bookie. Ralph thinks he ate the list to destroy the evidence. What does Ralph really eat?

A. a shopping list

B. a $50.00 bill

C. his Social Security card

D. the gas bill

9. On Christmas Eve, Ralph goes out to get some potato salad but returns with a police escort. Why is he almost arrested?

A. for crossing against the light in front of a police cruiser

B. for assaulting an officer

C. for breaking the delicatessen window

D. for stealing a loaf of bread

10. In "Lunchbox," Ralph wakes up the neighborhood while trying to think of an actress's name. What is the name of the police officer who comes to their apartment to tell them to keep it down?

A. Joe Callahan

B. Gallagher

C. Bill Casey

D. Jimmy Nolan

First Name Basis

SOME CHARACTERS ON *The Honeymooners* WERE KNOWN ONLY BY THEIR GIVEN NAMES. TEST YOUR FAMILIARITY WITH THESE SECOND-STRINGERS BY COMING UP WITH THEIR FIRST NAMES.

1. Rudy the Repairman's assistant

2. Lent his car to Joe the Thief

3. Charlotte Stattleman's jealous ex

4. Charlotte Stattleman's friend

5. Joe Malone's fiancée

6. Ex–Navy frogman turned sewer worker

7. Judy Connor's boyfriend

8. The Kramdens' maid

9. Coney Island fortune teller

10. Interior decorator for Morgan's

11. Trixie's role as a maid in a British TV commercial

12. Golf book dedication

13. Ralph's role in a 1956 Racoon Lodge play

14. Ed's role in a 1956 Racoon Lodge play

15. Alice's role in a 1956 Racoon Lodge play

16. Pool hall bully who picks a fight with Ralph

17. Pipsqueak pal of pool hall bully

18. *The $99,000 Answer* game show piano player

19. Ralph's disguise at the Festa L'Uva

20. Ed's disguise at the Festa L'Uva

21. Drove Danny and Bibbo's getaway car

22. Mr. Bartfeld's and Ralph's barber

23. Photographer for *Universal Magazine*

24. Sewer pal who borrows $2.00 from Ed to play dice

25. Songsmith's piano player

26. Audrey Meadows' dog

27. Alice's husband in Glow Worm advertisement

28. George the traffic manager's fiancée

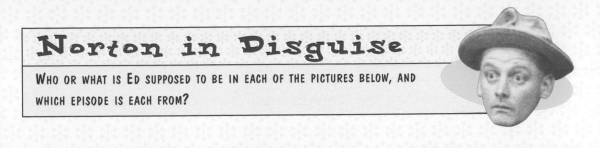

Norton in Disguise

WHO OR WHAT IS ED SUPPOSED TO BE IN EACH OF THE PICTURES BELOW, AND WHICH EPISODE IS EACH FROM?

1. _____
2. _____
3. _____
4. _____
5. _____

6. _____
7. _____
8. _____
9. _____

Triple Elimination

ELIMINATE THE EPISODES FROM THE LIST BELOW BY FOLLOWING EACH OF THESE RULES.
THE ORDER IN WHICH YOU GO THROUGH THE RULES DOES NOT CHANGE THE OUTCOME.

1. Eliminate three episodes in which Ed is the first main character we see, but Trixie isn't seen at all.

2. Eliminate three episodes in which we do not see Trixie at all, and Ralph does not wear his bus driver uniform.

3. Eliminate three episodes in which we see Ralph wearing his bus driver uniform, and Trixie is the first main character we see.

4. Eliminate three episodes in which Ralph is the first main character we see, and Ed does not wear his vest at all.

5. Eliminate three episodes in which Ed does not wear his vest, and the Kramdens' front door does not have a slide lock.

6. Eliminate three episodes in which the Kramdens' front door does not have a slide lock, and the doorknob is on the left side of the door.

7. Eliminate three episodes in which the doorknob is on the right side of the Kramdens' front door, and a fire escape can be seen right outside the kitchen window.

8. You should now be left with a single episode that can't be eliminated using any of the previous statements, and in which Ed is not seen at all.

"A Matter of Life and Death"

"Alice and the Blonde"

"Better Living Through TV"

"Catch a Star"

"Finders Keepers"

"Quiz Show"

"Halloween Party"

"Norton Moves In"

"Oh My Aching Back"

"One Big Happy Family"

"Income Tax Time"

"Ralph Kramden, Inc."

"Songs and Witty Sayings"

"Suspense"

"The Babysitter"

"The Cold"

"The Deciding Vote"

"The Great Jewel Robbery"

"The Safety Award"

"The Worry Wart"

"Dinner Guests"

"Honeymooners Christmas Show 1953"

Don't Touch Me, I'm Sterile

NOBODY LIKES GOING TO THE DOCTOR, LEAST OF ALL RALPH, BUT PUT YOUR MISGIVINGS ASIDE AND SEE IF YOU CAN CORRECTLY DIAGNOSE THE FOLLOWING MEDICAL MINDBENDERS.

1. Choose the best description for each of the following doctors.

A. DR. BRADY		TOOK BLOOD FROM RALPH FOR A TRANSFUSION
B. DR. DURGOM		BUS COMPANY PHYSICIAN
C. DR. STEVENS		VETERINARIAN
D. DR. FOLSOM		THE ONLY DOCTOR WHO CAN CURE ARTERIAL MONOCHROMIA
E. DR. HAMMOND		OBSTETRICIAN
F. DR. SEIFFER		A.K.A. "THE MAD BUTCHER OF BENSONHURST"
G. DR. MORTON		DIAGNOSED RALPH AND ED WITH THE MEASLES
H. DR. NORTON		TREATED ED AFTER A MANHOLE COVER FELL ON HIS HEAD

2. With what does the doctor inject Ed to get past his mental block and try to cure his sleepwalking?

3. The bus company sends Ralph to a psychiatrist because passengers are complaining about him being ill-tempered and insulting. What does the doctor diagnose as the problem, and what remedy does he suggest?

4. What is the name of the hypnotist whom Ralph brings home to hypnotize Alice?

5. Ed tells Ralph that Trixie made a doctor's appointment for Alice. This information combined with Ralph's finding baby clothes in the bureau leads him to believe that Alice is having a baby. What was Alice really going to the doctor for?

Game Show Showdown

RALPH HAS HAD MANY FRUITLESS OPPORTUNITIES TO GET HIS POT OF GOLD. ON *Beat the Clock* HE FINALLY WON SOMETHING, BUT HARDLY ENOUGH TO MAKE UP FOR ALL HE LOST OVER THE YEARS WITH HIS CRAZY SCHEMES. SEE HOW WELL YOU REMEMBER RALPH AND THE GANG'S ATTEMPTS AT GAME SHOW FAME AND FORTUNE.

1. Which of the following is NOT one of the ten category choices given to Ralph in "The $99,000 Answer"?
   A. Chinese Cooking   C. Women Behind the Men
   B. Rare Tropical Birds   D. Popular Movies

2. Which category does Ralph choose on *The $99,000 Answer* game show?

3. Who is the host of *The $99,000 Answer* game show?

4. What is the announcer's name on *The $99,000 Answer* game show?
   A. Tom   C. George
   B. Harry   D. Jose

5. In "The $99,000 Answer," how many questions must a contestant answer correctly to win $99,000.00?

6. In "The $99,000 Answer," which of the following songs does Ed NOT play on the piano while helping Ralph practice?
   A. "Shuffle Off to Buffalo"
   B. "Just Too Marvelous for Words"
   C. "Don't Fence Me In"
   D. "Swanee River"

7. Who is the host of *Beat the Clock*?

8. What is the assistant's name on *Beat the Clock*?
   A. Beverly   C. Roxanne
   B. Joyce   D. Sylvia

9. Fill in the blanks. In the first *Beat the Clock* challenge, Alice has to blow a _____ across a table using _____, and get it into a _____ that Ralph holds in his _____.

10. For their second challenge on *Beat The Clock*, Ralph and Alice have to "serve tea for two." Which of the following items is Alice responsible for?
    A. cups   C. lemons
    B. saucers   D. balloons

11. Ed takes Alice's place on *Beat the Clock*. What is the famous saying that he has to unscramble in the jackpot round?

12. How much cash and what prizes do Ralph, Alice, and Ed win on *Beat the Clock*?

13. What do the Kramdens get as a consolation prize on the *Krinkly Krax* quiz show?

14. The *Krinkly Krax* slogan is "The breakfast food that makes All-American boys." What does Ralph suggest they change this to?

15. Who gets the Kramdens on the *Krinkly Krax* quiz show?

16. Who is the quizmaster of the *Krinkly Krax* quiz show?

17. Ralph's first question on the *Krinkly Krax* quiz show is "Name a state west of the Mississippi." What is his answer?

18. After realizing that an error was made, the *Krinkly Krax* people go to the Kramdens' apartment to pose the jackpot question to Ralph: "What did Marconi invent?" What does he answer?

We're in Business

1. Match the name on the left with the type of business on the right.

A. Kelsey's	Pizzeria
B. Stellar	Drugstore
C. Wallace's	Candy store
D. Royal Hawaiian	Hotel
E. Harris'	Gym
F. Gerringer's	Gasoline station
G. Fascination	Department store
H. Salvatore's	Sporting goods store
I. Spiffy	Bar and grill
J. Fred's	Employment agency
K. Melacrina's	Bowling alley
L. Statler	Iron company
M. Bartfeld's	Motel

2. Match each of the names on the left with the corresponding descriptions on the right.

A. Dowser's on Dekalb Avenue	Ralph rented a tuxedo from here
B. Morgan's Department Store	The best place to get potato salad
C. Bloomgardens	Where Ralph bought a secondhand vacuum
D. Royal Chinese Gardens	The place where Ralph got a hot tip on a horse
E. Hong Kong Gardens	Redecorating the Kramdens' apartment free
F. McCloud's	Owned by Irving Shapiro
G. Devito's Delicatessen	Where Alice and Trixie bought the same dress
H. Krauss's Delicatessen	Alice likes their lychee nuts
I. Jerry's Lunchroom	The best place to get lasagna

Handy Housewife Helper

RALPH HAS FOUND ANOTHER SUREFIRE WAY TO MAKE SOME QUICK MONEY, AND POOR ED IS SUCKERED INTO IT. IN "BETTER LIVING THROUGH TV," THE TWO ENTREPRENEURS DECIDE TO GO ON TELEVISION TO SELL THE 2,000 HANDY HOUSEWIFE HELPER UTENSILS THAT THEY'VE GOTTEN HOLD OF. ALL GOES WELL TILL SHOW TIME. HERE'S A CHALLENGING SET OF QUESTIONS ABOUT THIS GOLDEN OPPORTUNITY THAT SANK LIKE A LEAD BALLOON.

1. How much are Ralph and Ed planning to charge for each Handy Housewife Helper?
   A. 50 cents   C. $1.50
   B. $1.00   D. $2.00

2. Taking into account the cost of the commercial and the purchase of the utensils, how much of a profit do Ralph and Ed expect to make?
   A. $800.00   C. $1,700.00
   B. $1,200.00   D. $1,800.00

3. According to Alice, how long would it take someone to sell all the Handy Housewife Helpers if they went door to door, and why?

4. How many times do Ralph and Ed rehearse their commercial before going on the air?
   A. once   C. fourteen times
   B. twice   D. fifteen times

5. Who plays the role of Chef of the Past, and who plays the Chef of the Future?

6. Ralph and Ed are scheduled for the _____ commercial break.
   A. first   C. third
   B. second   D. fourth

7. Ralph and Ed's commercial airs during a _____ movie.
   A. Charlie Chan   C. Jane Frazee
   B. Humphrey Bogart   D. Captain Video

8. Place the following tasks in the order in which they are to be performed in the commercial.
   A. coring an apple
   B. opening a can
   C. sharpening a knife

9. Where is the warehouse in which all the Handy Housewife Helpers are being stored?

10. Which of the following is NOT an attachment on the Handy Housewife Helper?
    A. corkscrew   C. glass cutter
    B. screwdriver   D. lock pick

Caller ID

In a few episodes, the phone number we hear does not correspond to the actor's lip movements. Apparently, the producers changed the numbers at a later time with a voiceover. But nobody's asking you to read lips here— question 1 refers to the numbers as heard.

1. Match the person or detail with the corresponding telephone number.

A. Ed and Trixie Norton	BEnsonhurst 5-6698
B. Evelyn Fensterblau	BEnsonhurst 0-7740
C. Charlotte Stattleman	BEnsonhurst 6-0099
D. Charlie Hartman	BEnsonhurst 0-7741
E. Number for ordering the Handy Housewife Helper	EVergreen 4-2598
F. The Kramdens' short-lived number	BEnsonhurst 6-0098
G. Number that Ralph called mistakenly thinking it was his own	MELrose-5099

2. In which two "Classic 39" episodes do the Kramdens have their own telephone?

3. Where is the telephone that Ralph uses to call "The Great Fatchoomara"?
A. in a luncheonette   C. on the street
B. in a barber shop   D. in Norton's apartment

4. In "Peacemaker," Ed runs away from home and goes to a malt shop, where he calls information. What phone number does he ask for?

5. In which of the following episodes do we NOT see a telephone booth inside the poolroom?
A. "The Next Champ"
B. "The Little Man Who Wasn't There"
C. "Trapped"
D. "The Great Jewel Robbery"

Twenty-three Skidoo

USING ONLY THE TWENTY-THREE WORDS LISTED HERE, FILL IN THE BLANKS TO COMPLETE THE EPISODE TITLES. SOME WORDS ARE USED MORE THAN ONCE, BUT NO MORE THAN THREE TIMES.

ALICE	ANNIVERSARY	AUNT	BOSS	CHRISTMAS	DOG
FAMILY	GOOD	GUEST	HOT	KRAMDEN	LETTER
LIFE	LOST	MAN	MATTER	NIGHT	NORTON
PARTY	RALPH	SWEET	TWO	YOUNG	

1. "_____'s _____ Ethel"

2. "_____ Speaker"

3. "_____ - _____ _____ Prince"

4. "Halloween _____ for the _____"

5. "_____'s Birthday"

6. "_____ vs. _____"

7. "_____ Gift"

8. "The Love _____"

9. "_____'s _____ Tooth"

10. "A _____'s _____"

11. "Honeymooners _____ Show 1953"

12. "_____ Plays Cupid"

13. "Halloween _____"

14. "Double _____"

15. "_____ to the _____"

16. "Brother _____"

17. "This Is Your _____"

18. "_____ - _____ Car"

19. "_____ _____, Inc."

20. "'Twas the _____ Before _____"

21. "_____ Baby"

22. "_____ _____ Stand"

23. "One Big Happy _____"

24. "_____ _____ with a Horn"

25. "_____ Tips"

26. "_____ Job"

27. "The Finger _____"

28. "_____ Bye _____ Ethel"

29. "A _____ of _____ and Death"

30. "_____ Men on a Horse"

31. "_____ at Heart"

32. "A _____ of Record"

33. "_____ Moves In"

34. "The Little _____ Who Wasn't There"

43

Number Cruncher

1. Ralph's candy bar commercial appears during the _____ performance of the Choosy Chews Symphony Hour.

A. 754th   C. 1,462nd
B. 1,218th   D. 1,621st

2. What are the lucky numbers that land Ralph $1,000.00 in a bread company's publicity campaign at a baseball game?

A. 2738   C. 4468
B. 3127   D. 5683

3. Ralph and Ed win a prize in the Teresa Grotta raffle. Ed says it's no wonder they won; his lucky number is on the raffle ticket. What is the ticket number?

A. 354
B. 827462
C. 4274610487
D. 2640933206988764322

4. Ralph's interview for a job as a street Santa is in which room of the Bellman Hotel?

A. 609   C. 421
B. 217   D. 513

5. What is the room number of the office that Ralph visits at *American Weekly Magazine* to sell his story about dying from arterial monochromia?

A. 1263   C. 1623
B. 2316   D. 2631

6. Ralph gets a hot tip that Cigar Box is going to win the eighth race at the track, but he ends up placing his bet on Happy Feet. What are the two horses' numbers?

7. Ralph puts $8.00 down on a pinball game. Ralph scores 67,000 points with his three balls, but his opponent wins with the first ball. What is his score?

A. 84,000   C. 98,000
B. 93,000   D. 112,000

8. In "Finders Keepers," Ralph's bus number and the address of the automat on 42nd Street are one and the same. What is the number?

9. The contestant before Ralph on *The $99,000 Answer* is asked the following question: "How many times does the figure 1 appear on a dollar bill either in numeral form or spelled out?" What is his (correct) reply?

10. Rudy the Repairman comes to fix the Kramdens' television set. What are the channel numbers that Alice is referring to in each of the following descriptions?
A. two channels that don't work while using the iron
B. two channels that don't work when a plane goes by
C. two channels that work all the time

11. Ralph makes a list of his faults and his good qualities. What does he list as fault 18?

12. Referring to the previous question, what does Ralph list as fault 22?

Family Album

Identify the following Kramden relatives by name and relation.

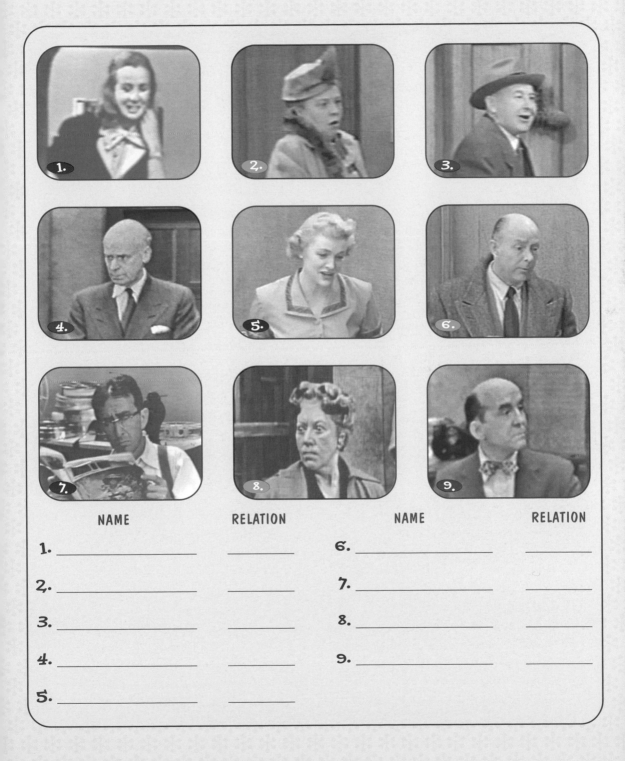

NAME	RELATION	NAME	RELATION
1. _____ _____		6. _____ _____	
2. _____ _____		7. _____ _____	
3. _____ _____		8. _____ _____	
4. _____ _____		9. _____ _____	
5. _____ _____			

"Classic 39" ID

HOW WELL DO YOU REMEMBER THE THIRTY-NINE SHOWS THAT WERE RERUN OVER AND OVER UNTIL THE MID-1980S? PROVE YOURSELF AN EXPERT BY NAMING EACH OF THESE "CLASSIC 39" EPISODES USING THE CLUES BELOW.

1. Ralph and Ed wear Racoon bowling team jackets.

2. Ed is going to the antique show at Madison Square Garden.

3. Ralph is seen wearing a cap from Martin Paints.

4. "Gee, I never knew Davy Crockett was so fat."

5. Ralph and Ed go to a boxing match at Madison Square Garden.

6. Alice and Trixie are playing mahjongg in the Nortons' apartment.

7. Ralph sews a chicken to his shirt.

8. Ralph is so shaken up he can't even cut bread.

9. Alice and Trixie wear the same dress.

10. Ralph and Ed are playing gin rummy.

11. Ralph polishes his socks.

12. Ralph sleeps on two chairs in the kitchen.

13. Ralph makes Ed wear an apron.

14. Ed locks Ralph out of the Kramdens' apartment.

15. Ralph is buying a motorboat with three propellers.

16. Ralph pricks his finger while handling a pincushion.

17. Ed is wearing a dress.

18. Ed burns Ralph's bowling jacket with an iron.

19. Mrs. Manicotti knocks all the dishes off her table.

20. "Boomf!"

21. Ralph climbs out of the bedroom window.

22. "Voh-doh-dee-oh-doh."

23. Alice is smoking a cigarette.

24. Ralph eats blueberry pie.

25. Norton gets a bump on his head from a fire escape ladder.

26. Teddy Oberman is looking through the Kramdens' icebox.

27. Ed sprinkles oatmeal on the Kramdens' kitchen floor.

28. Ralph sleeps in Norton's bedroom and Norton sleeps in the kitchen.

29. McGarrity says his picture will be in the newspaper for killing Ralph.

30. Ralph gets his fingers caught in a mousetrap.

31. The Kramdens and Nortons are seen sitting in a car.

32. Ed is using a typewriter.

33. Ralph hurts his hand on a punching bag.

34. Mr. Marshall is shooting pool.

35. Ed sprinkles rock candy on the Kramdens' floor.

36. Ralph asks Ed for a teensy-weensy piece of pizza.

37. Ed has been going to work an hour early for the past week.

38. The Kramdens have a typewriter on the kitchen table.

39. Ed's lunch floats away in the sewer.

"Letter to the Boss"

IN THIS LEGENDARY EPISODE, RALPH THINKS HE'S BEEN FIRED FROM THE BUS COMPANY. A MAN FROM THE SUPPLY ROOM HAS TOLD HIM TO TURN IN HIS UNIFORM BECAUSE HE WON'T BE DRIVING A BUS ANYMORE.

1. Ralph wants to write a letter to his boss to let him know what he thinks of him. He's too nervous to write the letter himself, so he dictates it to Ed. Fill in the blanks to complete the letter exactly as it was written by Ed.

Dear Mr. _____:
You dirty _____. You're nothing but a
miserable _____. You oughta turn
in your _____ card in the
_____ race. After firing me, after
_____ years, I could _____ say that
you are the _____ man in the whole
_____. You dirty _____.
_____ Yours,
_____ _____

2. After all the years of working for the bus company, what does Ralph say he has to show for it?

3. Alice removes the right sleeve from Ralph's undershirts because it's warm on the bus. Why doesn't she remove the left one?

4. Ralph finds out that he hasn't been fired. Instead, he's been promoted to _____.
A. dispatcher
B. assistant cashier
C. traffic manager
D. supervisor

5. A police officer overhears Ralph and Ed planning to get the letter out of a mailbox. What explanation does Ralph give the officer?

6. Where is the mailbox that Ralph and Ed want to break into?
A. in front of the bowling alley
B. in front of the pool hall
C. in front of the Kramdens' building
D. in front of the barber shop

7. The mailman catches Ralph and Ed lifting the mailbox. He says that the penalty for tampering with the mail is _____ years in jail or a $_____ fine.

8. Who is Ralph supposed to see about his new duties at the bus company?
A. Freddy Muller
B. Bill Johnson
C. Mr. Monahan
D. William Kalansky

Petrie Puzzler

GEORGE PETRIE WAS ONE OF THE MOST VERSATILE ACTORS ON *THE HONEYMOONERS*. HE COULD BE SEEN WEARING A SCAR OR A BEARD, AND PLAYED EVERYTHING FROM A CRIMINAL TO A RACOON. SEE HOW WELL YOU RECALL THE MANY NAMES AND OCCUPATIONS OF GEORGE PETRIE.

1. Name when he was the bus company doctor

2. Name in "Good Night Sweet Prince"

3. Name in "Catch a Star"

4. Occupation in "Income Tax Time"

5. Name in "Guest Speaker"

6. Occupation in "The Lawsuit"

7. Name in "The Next Champ"

8. Name in "Stand In for Murder"

9. Occupation in "Move Uptown"

10. Name in "Ralph's Sweet Tooth"

11. Name in "Teamwork Beat the Clock"

12. Occupation in "Brother-in-Law"

13. Name in "The Hypnotist"

14. Occupation in "The Hypnotist"

15. Name in "The Great Jewel Robbery"

16. Name in "Peacemaker"

17. Occupation in "The Adoption"

18. Occupation in "Songs and Witty Sayings"

19. Name in "Game Called on Account of Marriage"

20. Occupation in "Catch a Star" (two words)

21. Name in "The Lawsuit"

22. Occupation in "Stand In for Murder"

23. Occupation in "Ralph's Sweet Tooth"

24. Name in "Brother-in-Law"

25. Occupation in "Peacemaker"

26. Name in "Santa Claus and the Bookies"

27. Name in "Trapped"

Family Gossip

HERE ARE TWENTY STATEMENTS ABOUT THE KRAMDENS' AND NORTONS' EXTENDED FAMILIES. DETERMINE IF EACH IS TRUE OR FALSE. IF FALSE, SET THE RECORD STRAIGHT BY CORRECTING IT.

1. Ed's uncle George from Altoona sent Dynamite Moran to visit the Nortons.

2. When Ralph's cousin Louis passed away, his wife ran off to Atlantic City with the life insurance money.

3. All of Ralph's brothers are married.

4. Alice's brother, who is a lawyer, made up the ninety-nine-year lease that Norton signed in "My Fair Landlord."

5. In "Move Uptown," Ralph's brother Charlie was supposed to help the Kramdens move their furniture.

6. Ed Norton borrowed noisemakers left over from his father's fiftieth birthday party.

7. Alice's sister Grace is married to Stanley Saxon.

8. Trixie has a brother-in-law named Harvey.

9. Alice's sister Sally is married to Stanley Diamond.

10. Ed has a female cousin who is bald.

11. Ed has a cousin Gertrude who looks like Abe Lincoln.

12. Alice's sister Helen gave birth to twins.

13. Alice's aunt Kate attended the Kramdens' wedding.

14. Ralph used to work for the WPA with Alice's brother Freddie.

15. Alice has a sister who lives in the Bronx.

16. One of Ed's uncles went to school with Groucho Marx.

17. If Alice is making fish chowder it can only mean one thing: Her brother Frank is coming over for dinner.

18. Ralph's brother Harry owns a gas station with a car-washing machine.

19. Alice's brother Tom owns a filling station.

20. Ralph's mother has been yelling out of windows for eighty years, and eventually lost her voice.

Best Friends

HERE'S A SET OF QUESTIONS DEDICATED TO ONE OF THE MOST ENDURING FRIENDSHIPS OF ALL TIME.

1. When Ralph buys a two-family house, he suckers Ed into being his tenant and has him sign a ninety-nine-year lease. How old does Ed say he will be when the lease expires?

2. In "Oh My Aching Back," Ed offers to take Ralph's temperature. It turns out to be 111 degrees. Why?

3. Ed manages to electrocute Ralph in both "Vacation at Fred's Landing" and "One Big Happy Family." What was Ralph handling in each case?

4. For $20.00, Ed becomes vice president of the Ralph Kramden Corporation and owns _____ of the company stock.
   A. 25%   C. 35%
   B. 30%   D. 40%

5. In which episode from the 1950s do we see Ralph and Ed in jail?

6. In which episode does Ed cause Ralph to almost vacuum his lunch back out of his mouth?

7. Ralph and Ed celebrate their emancipation from jail by getting drunk on what they think is wine. What are they really drinking?

8. In "Kramden vs. Norton," Ralph wants to treat Ed to a movie for his birthday. Where does Ed take Ralph for his birthday that year?
   A. the Hong Kong Gardens   C. to a movie
   B. the Kit Kat Club   D. to a baseball game

9. In "Mind Your Own Business," Ed beats Ralph at gin rummy with 28,000 points. How much does Ralph owe him?
   A. 14 cents   C. $1.38
   B. 86 cents   D. $3.20

10. Ed once carried Ralph home piggyback from the bowling alley. What was wrong with Ralph?

11. In which of the following episodes do Ralph and Ed NOT sleep in the same bed/cot?
    A. "Unconventional Behavior"
    B. "Norton Moves In"
    C. "The Sleepwalker"
    D. "Hello, Mom"

12. In which episode do we see Ralph and Ed each faint twice?

13. True or false: When Ed's mother was sick, Ralph borrowed his brother's car to take Ed to New Jersey to visit her.

14. True or false: Ralph once punched Ed so hard that he knocked him out cold.

15. Complete the quote.
    Ed: "Now listen, Ralph, as long as we're neighbors you don't have to call me Norton. Call me _____."

51

Stage Fright

RALPH LIKES TO TAKE CENTER STAGE, BUT WHEN IT COMES TO CURTAIN TIME, HIS ANXIETY ALWAYS GETS THE BEST OF HIM. BREAK A LEG ANSWERING THIS SET OF STAGE STUMPERS.

1. Ralph "borrows" a numbing liquid from the dentist for his painful tooth, but it doesn't work when he applies it before going on the air to do a Choosy Chews commercial. Why?

2. How much is Ralph getting paid to be in the Choosy Chews commercial?
A. nothing
C. $100.00
B. $50.00
D. $200.00

3. Complete Ralph's line from the Choosy Chews commercial: "Remember, whether you're a _____ _____ or a _____ _____, eat Choosy Chews. It's _____ good candy."

4. Ralph is having a hard time remembering his lines for the Choosy Chews commercial. What is the name of the lady who writes the cue cards?
A. Margie
C. Josephine
B. Eleanor
D. Bridget

5. What is the name of the Choosy Chews Symphony's distinguished maestro?
A. Robert Miller
C. Wolfgang Becks
B. Hubble Budweiser
D. Ray Bloch

6. Before going on the air to do a Handy Housewife Helper commercial, Ed makes Ralph nervous by telling him that millions of people will be watching. Complete Ralph's response: "I wish you would stop _____ like that _____, you're going to get yourself all _____."

7. When the women's auxiliary of the Racoons put on a play, Ed tries to show off his acting abilities to Mr. Faversham by impersonating which famous actor?

8. After seeing her performance in the Racoons' play, which Hollywood producer wants to cast Alice in his next movie?

9. When _____ gets the flu, Ed Norton is called in to take his part in the Racoons' play because he fits the costume.
A. Joe Fensterblau
C. Joe Malone
B. Joe Munsey
D. Joe Hannigan

10. Ralph and Ed enter an amateur talent contest at the Halsey Theater with a comedy act, and Ed wants to tell a story about a farm. What is the title of the story, according to Ed?

11. What does Ed plan on doing with his share of the winnings from the Halsey Theater amateur talent contest?

12. Alice and Trixie decide to enter the Halsey Theater amateur talent contest. What will they be doing?

13. Ralph and Ed will be doing a Laurel and Hardy restaurant routine in their comedy act at the Halsey Theater. What type of pie does Laurel (Ed) ask for, and what type of pie does Hardy (Ralph) offer instead?

14. When the host of *The $99,000 Answer* asks a nervous Ralph what he does for a living, what does Ralph answer?

Dimwit Ed

WHAT ED NORTON LACKS IN INTELLIGENCE, HE MAKES UP FOR WITH HIS HEART OF GOLD. TEST YOUR KNOWLEDGE AGAINST ED'S WITH THE FOLLOWING NORTONISMS.

1. Ed (trying to cheer up Ralph): "Doctors can be wrong, too. Take a friend of mine—the doctor told him that he had six months to live. Boy, did he make a monkey out of that doctor." What happened?

2. Man from *American Weekly*: "Tell me, Dr. Norton, where do you practice medicine?" What is Ed's reply?

3. How does Ed spell the word "beauty"?

4. Ed (trying to give Ralph ideas on how to get out of going to dinner with Bill Davis): "Tell him you got a new job—that you're captain of the _____, and the ship is sailing in twenty minutes."

5. How does Ed answer this question on his civil service exam: "If you were heating your own home and oil was 12 cents a gallon and it went up 7%, and coal at the same time was $14.00 a ton, and that went up 9%, what would you do?"

6. Ed is rehearsing for a Racoons' play. Complete the following line.
Ed: "I don't possess a mansion, a villa in France, a yacht, or a string of _____."

7. Ralph and Ed are practicing a mind-reading act. Ralph holds up a hat and gives Ed the following clue: "This might be a little over your head." What are Ed's two guesses about the object?

8. When Ralph thinks the IRS is investigating his taxes, Ed tries to help by telling Ralph to stand on which constitutional amendment?

9. The Racoons want to hire a celebrity in an effort to sell more tickets to their annual dance. How does Ed suggest they come up with the money?

10. In "Stand In for Murder," Ed is helping Alice by stirring what he thinks is cake mix, and he decides to have a taste. What is Alice preparing in the bowl?

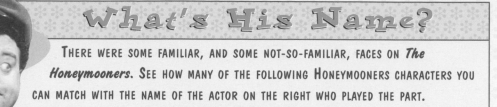

What's His Name?

THERE WERE SOME FAMILIAR, AND SOME NOT-SO-FAMILIAR, FACES ON *The Honeymooners*. SEE HOW MANY OF THE FOLLOWING HONEYMOONERS CHARACTERS YOU CAN MATCH WITH THE NAME OF THE ACTOR ON THE RIGHT WHO PLAYED THE PART.

1. McGarrity ("The $99,000 Answer")   Boris Aplon

2. Teddy Oberman ("Pal o' Mine")   Dick Bernie

3. Mr. Bartfield ("The Babysitter")   Ronnie Burns

4. Dick Prescott ("Head of the House")   Alexander Clark I

5. Pete Woodruff ("The Man From Space")   Les Damon

6. Train Conductor ("Unconventional Behavior")   Humphrey Davis

7. Barney Hacket ("Stand In for Murder")   Ned Glass

8. Bill Davis ("A Man's Pride")   John Griggs I

9. Freddy Muller ("Classic 39")   Eddie Hanley

10. Carlos Sanchez ("Mama Loves Mambo")   Charles Korvin

11. Wallace ("Young at Heart")   Frank Marth

12. Mr. Johnson ("Dial J for Janitor")   George Petrie

13. J.J. Marshall ("Opportunity Knocks But")   Sid Raymond

14. Herbert J. Whiteside ("On Stage")   Luis Van Rooten

15. Mr. Tebbetts ("A Dog's Life")   Bill Zuckert

The Gotham Bus Company

NEITHER RAIN, NOR SLEET, NOR GLOOM OF NIGHT CAN KEEP RALPH FROM SWIFTLY DELIVERING THE MAILMAN TO HIS APPOINTED ROUNDS. SEE HOW YOU FARE UNRAVELING THESE KNOTTY QUESTIONS ABOUT RALPH'S PLACE OF EMPLOYMENT.

1. What is the street address of the Gotham Bus Company?

2. Match each of the following bus company employees with his or her job description:

A) Mr. Butler   Bus Driver

B) Dutch   Claims Adjuster

C) Miss Wilson   Dispatcher

D) Joe Malone   Doctor

E) John J. Marshall Payroll

F) Freddie Muller   President

G) Frank Ferguson Vice President

H) Agres   Secretary

I) Mr. Douglas   Traffic Manager

3. What is Ralph's badge number?

4. How many times has Ralph's bus been held up?

5. What are the numbers of the two buses Ralph drives?

6. In which episode does Ralph mistakenly feed dog food to his boss?

Mother-in-Law

1. When Ralph gets tickets to a murder mystery play, his mother-in-law blabs the surprise ending and ruins it. According to Ralph's alarm clock, how long is she in the house before spilling the beans?
   A. two minutes
   B. three minutes
   C. four minutes
   D. five minutes

2. Which neighbor tells Mrs. Gibson about the ending to "Murder Strikes Out"?
   A. Mrs. Hannan
   B. Mrs. Stevens
   C. Mrs. Connors
   D. Mrs. Finley

3. When Alice's mother hears that Ralph found a lot of money on the bus, she sweet-talks him into giving her $200.00. What does she want to do with the money?

4. Mr. Marshall lies about being sick so that he doesn't have to go to his mother-in-law's house for New Year's Eve. Where do he and Mrs. Marshall go?

5. What special occasion does Alice's mother assume that Ralph has forgotten in "The Great Jewel Robbery"?

6. In "A Matter of Record," Mrs. Gibson complains that the Kramdens live _____ long blocks away from the subway.
   A. three
   B. five
   C. six
   D. eight

7. Ralph thinks his mother-in-law is coming to visit and has a big fight with Alice, which results in Ralph's sleeping in Norton's apartment. Who really comes to visit them?

8. Ralph wants to participate in the bowling championship, but Alice wants Ralph to go to her mother's house for a family get-together to see which visiting relative?

9. In which episode does Ralph call his mother-in-law a blabbermouth to her face?
   A. "Hello, Mom"
   B. "A Matter of Record"
   C. "The Great Jewel Robbery"
   D. "Oh My Aching Back"

10. Complete the following excerpt from a letter, which was written by Ralph to his mother-in-law.
    "A mother-in-law is the most _____, the most _____, and the most _____ of all women."

Facts about Norton

TEST YOUR KNOWLEDGE ABOUT ED NORTON WITH THESE TRICKY MINDBENDERS.

1. Which of the following materials is Ed allergic to?
A. polyester   C. cashmere
B. crinoline   D. rayon

2. What was Ed's major in vocational school?
A. arithmetic   C. plumbing
B. typing   D. French

3. Ed studied _____ under the GI bill.
A. arithmetic   C. plumbing
B. typing   D. French

4. What is Ed's favorite sourball flavor?
A. Cherry   C. Lime
B. Orange   D. Lemon

5. Ed has taken up bird watching. What type of bird does he see while eating lunch with Ralph in the park?
A. a blue-headed robin
B. a chicken hawk
C. a yellow-bellied sapsucker
D. none of the above

6. When Ralph records his apology to Alice on a vinyl record, Ed offers to play some background music on the harmonica. What song does Ed play?

7. Ed was once on a quiz show, but he couldn't even answer the first question. What was the question, and why couldn't he answer it?

8. Match each of the following shirts that Ed wears under his vest with the corresponding episode.   "The Next Champ"
A. white T-shirt   "Quiz Show"
B. black T-shirt   "Lost Job"
C. white sleeveless undershirt   "Funny Money"
D. white button-down dress shirt

9. Ed gets fired from the sewer after he pulls the ol' squeeze play on his boss per Ralph's advice. How long had Ed been working in the sewer at the time?
A. twelve years   C. fifteen years
B. fourteen years   D. seventeen years

10. In "Head of the House," Ed reveals to us that he goes shopping with Trixie every _____ afternoon.
A. Wednesday   C. Saturday
B. Friday   D. Sunday

1. When Alice has a telephone installed in the Kramden apartment, she decides to take on a baby-sitting job to help pay for it. Her first job is for Mr. and Mrs. Bartfeld. What is their address?
A. 33 Kosciusko Street
B. 383 Himrod Street
C. 465 Van Buren Street
D. 6409 Park Avenue

2. Alice's second baby-sitting job is for Mr. and Mrs. Wahlstetter. What is their address?
A. 33 Kosciusko Street
B. 383 Himrod Street
C. 465 Van Buren Street
D. 6409 Park Avenue

3. What is Mr. and Mrs. Gibson's address?
A. 33 Kosciusko Street
B. 383 Himrod Street
C. 465 Van Buren Street
D. 6409 Park Avenue

4. When Ralph lands a job with an "insurance company," they give him a lush apartment on Park Avenue. What is his new apartment number?
A. 13 D   C. 17 A
B. 21 B   D. 12 C

5. When Ralph and Ed get a job as a street Santa and his elf, at what street intersection are they supposed to work?
A. DeKalb and Flatbush avenues
B. 42nd Street and Columbus Avenue
C. Madison Avenue and 48th Street
D. 8th and Montgomery streets

6. Ralph and Ed cause a riot at an automat while looking for a $1,000.00 bill in a contest. Where is the automat located?
A. 42nd Street   C. Columbus Circle
B. Fifth Avenue   D. Chauncey Street

7. On what street does Ralph most commonly drive his bus?
A. Lexington Avenue   C. Madison Avenue
B. Fifth Avenue   D. Park Avenue

8. On what street is the Royal Chinese Gardens restaurant located?
A. DeKalb Avenue
B. Flatbush Avenue
C. Himrod Street
D. Chauncey Street

9. Besides monetary compensation, Ralph's pension includes a lifetime pass for two on the _____ bus.
A. Madison Avenue
B. Chauncey Street
C. Fifth Avenue
D. River Street

10. Ed plans on attending the Racoons' annual costume party but gets called to work on an emergency in the _____ sewer.
A. Himrod Street   C. 42nd Street
B. 225th Street   D. Madison Avenue

Rendezvous

GET OUT YOUR DATE BOOK AND SEE IF YOU CAN VERIFY THE TIMES, DATES, AND PLACES OF THE APPOINTMENTS MENTIONED IN THIS QUIZ.

1. MATCH THE FOLLOWING APPOINTMENTS WITH THE CORRESPONDING TIME AND PLACE.

APPOINTMENT	DATE AND/OR TIME	PLACE
A. DYNAMITE MORAN'S FIGHT ROOM IS SCHEDULED FOR	9:30 P.M.	COLONNADE
B. RALPH HAS TO MEET RICHARD PUTER	FRIDAY AT 8:00 P.M.	MONTGOMERY STREET
C. THE KRAMDENS ARE MEETING MR. AND MRS. DAVIS	A WEEK FROM FRIDAY AT 6:00 P.M.	KELSEY'S GYM
D. RALPH IS RECEIVING HIS SAFETY AWARD	6:00 P.M.	LAUREL GARDENS
E. RALPH IS SUPPOSED TO FIGHT WITH HARVEY	THE 21ST OF THE MONTH AT 10:00 A.M.	IRS OFFICE
F. RALPH STARTS WORKING AS A STREET SANTA	12:30 P.M.	CITY HALL

2. Ralph has to be at Mrs. Mary Monahan's apartment at 10:00 a.m. Friday _____.
A. for dinner
B. for the reading of her will
C. to sign a lease to his new apartment
D. for the boss's engagement party

3. In "Champagne and Caviar," after inviting his boss to dinner, Ralph is asked to meet Mr. Marshall in his office at 10:00 a.m. sharp to discuss _____.
A. a promotion
B. a raise
C. how well a bus driver can live on his current salary
D. a change in Ralph's bus route

4. Ralph has set up a blind date between Herman Gruber and Charlotte Stattleman. Where will they be meeting?
A. at Charlotte's apartment
B. at the Kramdens' apartment
C. at Herman's apartment
D. in front of the Halsey Theater

5. Ralph lies to Bill Davis about being boss of the bus company, and now Bill wants to meet Ralph at Ralph's office. Whose office does Ralph borrow?
A. Mr. Marshall's   C. Mr. Muller's
B. Mr. Monahan's   D. Mr. Johnson's

6. In "Santa and the Bookies," Trixie makes an appointment for Alice to see a doctor because her sacroiliac is acting up. On what day is her appointment?
A. Monday   C. Friday
B. Wednesday   D. Saturday

One of these Days, Alice...

HERE'S A SET OF STUMPERS DESIGNED TO TEST HOW MUCH YOU REALLY KNOW ABOUT RALPH'S FAVORITE LITTLE REDHEAD.

1. When is Alice Kramden's birthday?

2. What is Alice's maiden name?

3. Which girl scout troop was Alice a member of when she was a child?

4. How many of Alice's ex-boyfriends are named in the "Classic 39" episodes?
A. 2   C. 6
B. 4   D. 8

5. In which two episodes from the 1950s does Alice rehearse lines for a play she is performing in?

6. Which one of the following is not a job that Alice has had?
A. Laundry worker   B. Grocery clerk
C. Babysitter   D. Riveter

7. What color are Alice's eyes?

8. In "New Year's Eve Party," what are Alice's three New Year's resolutions?

9. Which grade school did Alice attend?

10. In which episode does Alice have a job as a receptionist for an obstetrician?

Show Me the Money

WHEN THEY'RE NOT SPENDING THEIR MONEY SHOOTING POOL OR BOWLING, RALPH AND ED ARE BUSY FINDING OTHER WAYS TO LOSE A BUCK. THIS QUIZ SHOULD TEST JUST HOW MUCH YOU KNOW ABOUT WHERE THE KRAMDENS' AND NORTONS' MONEY ENDS UP.

1. How much does Ralph spend on boxing equipment when he takes on the job of managing Dynamite Moran?

A. $20.00
B. $40.00
C. $60.00
D. $100.00

2. Who offers Ralph and Ed $750.00 to buy Dynamite Moran's contract?

A. Herb Armstrong
B. Jack Philbin
C. John Marshall
D. Slugger Simpson

3. Alice has purchased life insurance for herself and Ralph. Where is she getting the money for it?

A. she's taking it out of the grocery money
B. she's taking it out of the laundry money
C. she's getting a part-time job
D. she's taking it from her allowance

4. Alice stashes away $10.00, but Ralph spends it on jellybeans trying to win a contest. What was Alice saving the money for?

A. Christmas presents
B. furniture
C. Ralph's birthday present
D. a dress

5. At this writing, it costs $1.50 to ride the New York City subway. According to Alice, how much did it cost in December of 1953?

A. 10 cents
B. 15 cents
C. 25 cents
D. 40 cents

6. When the Kramdens go to dinner with the Davises, neither couple has enough money to pay the check themselves, but together they are able to cover it. Match each person with the amount of money he or she contributes.

A. Ralph $9.00
B. Alice $12.00
C. Bill $7.00
D. Millie $16.00

7. How much money has Ed saved up for the Racoons' Chicago convention?

A. $75.00
B. $100.00
C. $125.00
D. $200.00

8. Alice stashes away $180.00, and Ralph wants it so he can go to the Racoons' convention in Chicago. What does Alice want the money for?

A. their old age
B. Christmas presents
C. new furniture
D. a rainy day

9. The Kramdens and Nortons buy a summer cottage, which turns out to be a dump. They sell it at an $11.00 profit to Mr. Wahlstetter, but later find out that he plans to sell the cottage to highway developers for _____.

A. $2,000.00
B. $2,500.00
C. $3,000.00
D. $4,000.00

10. On his 1955 tax returns, Ralph deducts $80.00 he has spent throughout the year entertaining _____ whenever there was an opening for a traffic manager's position at the bus company.

A. Freddie Muller
B. Mr. Marshall
C. Mr. Douglas
D. Mr. Monahan

Howdy, Neighbor

GOOD NEIGHBORS ARE HARD TO COME BY, AND THE HONEYMOONERS ARE NO EXCEPTION. TRY TO ANSWER THESE QUESTIONS ABOUT THE JOYS AND SORROWS OF LIVING IN A CROWDED METROPOLIS.

1. Ralph bites off more than he can chew when he takes a job as janitor of the Chauncey Street building. Match each resident with the corresponding complaint he or she makes to Ralph.

   A. Mrs. Bennett   Bathtub needs fixing

   B. Mrs. Olsen   Doesn't have any water

   C. Mrs. Hanlon   Bathroom sink needs fixing

   D. Mrs. Manicotti   Something is missing out of her icebox

   E. Mrs. Fogarty   Venetian blinds are broken

   F. Mr. Riley   Radiator doesn't work

   G. Ed Norton   "Eureka, my garbage can is full"

2. Who lives next door to the Kramdens before Carlos Sanchez moves in?
   A. Mr. Fogarty   C. Mr. Schwartz
   B. Mr. Garrity   D. Mr. Riley

3. In "The Songwriters," which neighbor disturbs Ralph and Ed's attempts at songwriting by running a vacuum cleaner?
   A. Mrs. Stevens   C. Mrs. Norton
   B. Mrs. Manicotti   D. Mrs. Garrity

4. Who moves into the Chauncey Street building first, the Kramdens or the Nortons?

5. In "Young at Heart," which of the following neighbors has a date with Wallace?
   A. Millicent Brady   C. Charlotte Stattleman
   B. Judy Connors   D. Angelina Manicotti

6. In "Move Uptown," Ralph and Alice plan on moving to an apartment in the Bronx. Who will be their new landlord?
   A. Mr. Lewis   C. Mr. Rogers
   B. Mr. Johnson   D. Mr. Dennehy

7. Who is the blabbermouth who looks at everyone's gas bill and "yackety-yaks" all over the building?
   A. Mrs. Gallagher   C. Mrs. Helprin
   B. Mrs. Cassidy   D. Mrs. Schwartz

8. In "Trapped," which young neighbor forgets his water pistol in the Kramdens' apartment?
   A. Jimmy Doyle   C. Tommy Manicotti
   B. Johnny Bennett   D. Eddie Hodges

9. Which young neighbor visits the Kramdens on Christmas Eve to sing a song?
   A. Jimmy Doyle   C. Tommy Manicotti
   B. Johnny Bennett   D. Eddie Hodges

10. In "Lunchbox," Ed leans out the Kramdens' window to try to read the movie theater marquee up the street, but a neighbor's long underwear is blocking the view. Whose underwear is it?
    A. Mr. Manicotti's   C. Mr. Garrity's
    B. Mr. Murphy's   D. Mr. Flaherty's

Moving Out

In several episodes we saw the Kramdens and Nortons pack their bags and attempt to move. Whether they actually moved out or not, they always ended up back on Chauncey Street. See how fast you can move through these challenging questions.

1. When the Kramdens buy a two-family home and take the Nortons in as tenants, Ed voices a few complaints to Ralph about the apartment. Which of the following is NOT a problem mentioned by Ed?
A. The front door doesn't lock.
B. The door on the bedroom closet doesn't open.
C. The door on the kitchen closet doesn't close.
D. The hall closet doesn't have a door.

2. In "My Fair Landlord," Ed's lease states that he cannot throw a party unless he does what?

3. In "My Fair Landlord," Ed wants his apartment painted specific colors. For the walls he wants a color "like when the setting sun in Coney Island is striking the mustard, which reflects onto the hotdog through the sauerkraut." What color is he describing?

4. Ed wants Ralph to paint the moldings and window frames "the color of Ricardo Cortez's corneas in a Technicolor movie." What color is he describing?

5. What color does Ralph say he's going to paint Ed's apartment?

6. In "Move Uptown," the Kramdens plan on moving to the Bronx. Who are the current tenants of the apartment that Ralph has found?

7. Where are the Bronx apartment's current tenants moving to?

8. What must the Kramdens do before they can move into their new apartment in the Bronx?

9. In "One Big Happy Family," the Kramdens and Nortons rent an apartment together. Where do they move to?

10. In "One Big Happy Family," what does Ralph put between two pieces of toast that he tries to make Ed eat?

11. How much is the monthly rent for the Kramdens' and Nortons' shared apartment?

12. In "One Big Happy Family," what does Ed play with in the bathtub?
A. a rubber ducky   C. a boat
B. Captain Video figurines   D. a frogman

13. In "One Big Happy Family," Ralph tries to listen to the radio but Ed wants to watch television. What show is Ed watching?

14. In "Cottage For Sale," Ralph and Ed buy a country cottage together. What is the name of the complex in which their cottage is located?

Last Name Scramble

UNSCRAMBLE THE LAST NAME OF EACH PERSON IDENTIFIED IN THE CLUES BELOW.

1. I asked Ralph to sign a petition to build a new playground in the neighborhood.
Miss LASTNAMES

2. I was the Kramdens' and Nortons' superintendent in Flushing, Queens, for a short time.
Mr. MERGI

3. I'm one of the superintendents at the Chauncey Street apartment.
Mr. NOSLE

4. I told Alice about a baby-sitting job.
Mrs. NIPSSMO

5. I'm the Kramdens' and Nortons' landlord.
Mr. SHONONJ

6. I'm the eviction lawyer who got evicted from my own office.
Sam MIGSWAG

7. I asked if I could call New Jersey on the house phone that Ralph installed in the building.
Mrs. CSZWRATH

8. I'm the reporter from *Universal Magazine* who did a story on Ralph's safety record.
Mr. NATRIM

9. I was the contestant who appeared on *The $99,000 Answer* before Ralph.
Mr. KRAPER

10. I was the late Mary Monahan's maid.
Mary L'NOODLEN

11. I was the late Mary Monahan's butler.
Herbert SOMBAC

12. I was the late Mary Monahan's estate lawyer.
Frederick NASCOR

13. I'm the late Mary Monahan's nephew.
Robert H. RYEBALD

14. I am the secretary at the Stellar Employment Agency.
Miss DRYNOSEL

15. I am the publisher of *American Weekly Magazine*.
Dick CRESGH

16. I won $8.00 playing pinball against Ralph.
Bill SORMIR

17. I'm in the automobile parts business and Ralph introduced me to my wife.
Charlie MARANTH

18. I'm the questioning photographer who wrote about Ralph being the king of his castle.
Dick ECTSPORT

19. I knocked out Dynamite Moran in the Kramdens' apartment.
Mr. ORALTY

20. I bet Ralph that he couldn't get Alice to cook me a nice dinner.
Joe TUNELEBARFS

Wall of Fame

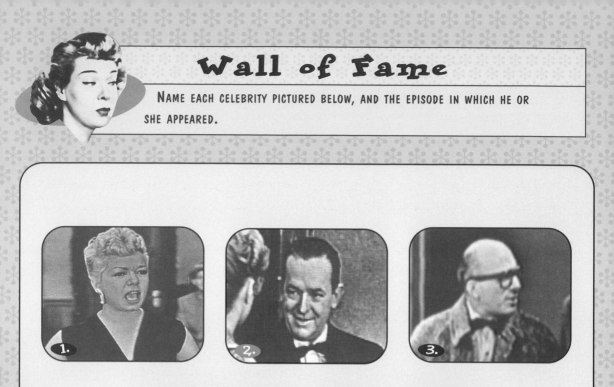

Name each celebrity pictured below, and the episode in which he or she appeared.

CELEBRITY NAME   EPISODE TITLE

1. _____   _____

2. _____   _____

3. _____   _____

4. _____   _____

5. _____   _____

Fact or Fiction?

Is each of the following statements a fact, or were they just made up by the writers? Test your expertise by answering "fact" or "fiction" for each statement.

1. Not only was Bud Collyer the host of *Beat the Clock* on *The Honeymooners*, he was also the host of the real television game show of the same name.

2. *Captain Video and His Video Rangers* was a real television program.

3. The Gotham Bus Company was the name of New York City's surface transit line in the 1950s.

4. Chauncey Street is a real street in Bensonhurst, Brooklyn.

5. Jackie Gleason got his start in show business through an amateur night competition at the Halsey Theater.

6. *The $99,000 Answer* was a real game show in the 1950s.

7. The New York Giants really won the World Series on the day that "Game Called on Account of Marriage" was broadcast.

8. In "The Songwriters," Ralph and Ed write a song called "My Love Song to You." This is a real song recorded by Bob Manning.

9. The Watchung Mountains overlook Lake Pokamoonshine in New Jersey, therefore it is possible that Fred's Landing really existed.

10. In "Game Called on Account of Marriage," Stanley is eloping with Alice's sister Sally. The actor and actress playing the roles of Stanley and Sally were really married to each other.

11. The Kramdens and Nortons go to the movies to see *Burning Lips*. This was a real movie from the 1950s.

12. In "Catch a Star," Ralph and Ed go to the Park Sheraton Hotel to find Jackie Gleason. This was where most of *The Honeymooners* episodes were filmed.

Seeing Double

WHILE USUALLY CAUSED BY A LUMP ON THE NOGGIN OR A FEW TOO MANY MARTINIS FOR BREAKFAST, YOU MIGHT JUST GET DOUBLE VISION FROM ANSWERING THE QUESTIONS IN THIS QUIZ.

1. Select the two episodes in which Ed is seen wearing a dress.
   A. "Better Living Through TV"
   B. "A Woman's Work Is Never Done"
   C. "Halloween Party"
   D. "A Man's Pride"

2. Select the two episodes in which Ed is seen sleepwalking.
   A. "Good Night Sweet Prince"
   B. "Oh My Aching Back"
   C. "The Sleepwalker"
   D. "The Hypnotist"

3. Select the two episodes in which we see a towel labeled "Hers" in the Kramden apartment.
   A. "Lost Baby"
   B. "Good Night Sweet Prince"
   C. "Ralph's Sweet Tooth"
   D. "Dinner Guests"

4. In "The Little Man Who Wasn't There," a man who could be Ed Norton's double enters the Kramden apartment. Who is he?
   A. Ed's brother
   B. Ed's cousin
   C. a new neighbor
   D. a delivery boy

5. Select the two episodes in which we see Trixie dressed as a sailor.
   A. "Songs and Witty Sayings"
   B. "On Stage"
   C. "Cupid"
   D. "Halloween Party"

6. Select the two episodes in which Ralph and Ed try to make a baby-bottle nipple out of a rubber glove.
   A. "Expectant Fathers"
   B. "The Adoption"
   C. "Lost Baby"
   D. "The Babysitter"

7. Select the two episodes in which Alice receives a hairpin box made of 2,000 matches as a gift.
   A. "Honeymooners Christmas Show 1953"
   B. "Alice's Birthday"
   C. "'Twas the Night Before Christmas"
   D. "Anniversary Gift"

8. Select the two episodes in which Ed is warming up on the piano with "Swanee River."
   A. "Songwriters"
   B. "The $99,000 Answer"
   C. "On Stage"
   D. "Songs and Witty Sayings"

9. Select the two episodes in which the Kramdens have a television set in their apartment.
   A. "Better Living Through TV"
   B. "Funny Money"
   C. "Champagne and Caviar"
   D. "Honeymooners Christmas Show 1953"

10. Select the two episodes in which the Kramdens have a modern refrigerator in their apartment.
    A. "Champagne and Caviar"
    B. "The Adoption"
    C. "Funny Money"
    D. "Ralph Kramden, Inc."

Matchmaker

MATCH EACH OF THE FOLLOWING MEN ON THE LEFT WITH HIS CORRECT SPOUSE, GIRLFRIEND, OR FIANCÉE. EACH NAME ON THE RIGHT MAY BE USED MORE THAN ONCE.

1. Joe Malone

2. Herman Gruber

3. John J. Marshall

4. Judge Lawrence Norton Hurdle

5. George (the bus company traffic manager)

6. Burt Wedemeyer

7. Bill Davis

8. Freddie Zimmerman

9. Stanley Saxon

10. Stanley Diamond

11. Joe Manicotti

12. Harvey Wahlstetter

13. Walter Jensen

14. Ralph Kramden Sr.

15. Ralph Kramden Jr.

16. Edward L. Norton

17. Alice's uncle Leo

18. Alice's brother-in-law Jerry

19. Freddie Muller

CHARLOTTE

THELMA

AGNES

GLADYS

HARRIET

RITA

ALICE

HENRIETTA

SARAH

DOROTHY

ANGELINA

SALLY

ETHEL

MILLIE

ELIZABETH

HELEN

Scenic Recall

THE KRAMDENS' APARTMENT WAS THE MOST POPULAR LOCALE USED IN *The Honeymooners*, BUT IT CERTAINLY WASN'T THE ONLY ONE. CAN YOU RECALL IN WHICH EPISODE EACH OF THE FOLLOWING SCENES TOOK PLACE? THERE IS ONLY ONE CORRECT MATCHING ANSWER FOR EACH.

1. INSIDE JACK PHILBIN'S OFFICE   "CUPID"

2. INSIDE ADELE PATERSON'S OFFICE   "THIS IS YOUR LIFE"

3. INSIDE DR. DURGOM'S OFFICE   "VACATION AT FRED'S LANDING"

4. INSIDE A PSYCHIATRIST'S OFFICE   "NEW YEAR'S EVE PARTY WITH THE DORSEYS"

5. INSIDE CAFÉ ROUGE   "THE SLEEPWALKER"

6. INSIDE PIETRO AND COLUCHI GROTTO'S RESTAURANT   "CATCH A STAR"

7. INSIDE THE HALSEY THEATER   "THE LOVE LETTER"

8. OUTSIDE THE HALSEY THEATER   "SANTA CLAUS AND THE BOOKIES"

9. INSIDE A HOSPITAL WAITING ROOM   "BATTLE OF THE SEXES"

10. INSIDE THE BUS COMPANY LOCKER ROOM   "THE GREAT JEWEL ROBBERY"

11. INSIDE CHARLOTTE STATTLEMAN'S APARTMENT   "RALPH'S SWEET TOOTH"

12. INSIDE BURT WEDEMEYER'S APARTMENT   "STARS OVER FLATBUSH"

'Tis the Season

1. Match the following gifts with the gift giver and receiver in "'Twas the Night Before Christmas":

GIFT	GIVER	RECEIVER
A. Spats	Alice	Ralph and Alice
B. Necktie	Alice	Ralph
C. $25.00 gift certificate	Mrs. Stevens	Mrs. Stevens
D. Pajamas	Uncle Leo	Alice
E. Bowling ball bag	Ralph	Ed
F. Hairpin box	Mrs. Gibson	Ralph
G. Kitchen thermometer	Ed	Ralph

2. In "Honeymooners Christmas Party," name the six roles played by Jackie Gleason.

3. Who gets the same present in both "Honeymooners Christmas Show 1953" and "'Twas the Night Before Christmas," and what is it?

4. Fill in the blanks. In "'Twas the Night Before Christmas," Ed tells Ralph, "Compared to you, Scrooge was a _____ _____."

Who Am I?

USING THE "LOST EPISODES" AS YOUR GUIDE, SEE IF YOU CAN IDENTIFY THE PERSON WHO COULD MAKE EACH OF THE FOLLOWING CLAIMS.

1. I'm the best street fighter Ed Norton has ever seen.

2. I'm the Racoon Lodge member who is a fight promoter.

3. I'm Jimmy and Tommy Dorsey's manager.

4. I had to drive a bus on the Fourth of July, Thanksgiving, Christmas, and New Year's Eve.

5. I'm chairman of the raffle committee for the Teresa Grotta Service League.

6. I was Ralph and Alice's daughter, if for only a short while.

7. Fenwick delivered my keg of beer to the Kramdens' apartment by mistake.

8. I used to hang out at the pool hall, but when my little dog got sick, I went nuts and they put me away.

9. I was the lemon machine.

10. Ralph and Alice couldn't think of my name after seeing me in a movie.

11. I owe Ed Norton a favor because he saved me from drowning in the sewer.

12. I work behind the cigar counter at the drugstore.

13. Ralph set me up on a blind date with his grade-school friend.

14. If Ed Norton had married me, he would be driving his own garbage truck for a living.

15. I bet $10.00 on Rocking Chair to win the horse race in Florida.

16. Ralph told his future brother-in-law that I was in love with Alice's sister, in an effort to get them to elope.

17. I used to work with Ed in the sewer, but now I'm the orchestra leader on the *Robert Q. Lewis Show*.

18. We forgot our sheet music in a telephone booth, but Alice found it and returned it.

19. Ralph asked me for my autograph at the Park Sheraton Hotel.

20. Ralph invited me over to watch his fighter work out.

The Kramdens

THEY HAVE THEIR FIGHTS. THEY ARGUE AT ALL HOURS OF THE NIGHT AND DAY. BUT IN THE END, THEY ALWAYS SEEM TO WORK IT OUT. HERE'S YOUR CHANCE TO PROVE YOU KNOW WHY IT'S A HAPPY ENDING EVERY TIME FOR EVERYONE'S FAVORITE COUPLE FROM BENSONHURST.

1. Where do Ralph and Alice go dancing on their first date?

2. Where do Ralph and Alice go for their honeymoon?
A. Atlantic City
B. Niagara Falls
C. Fred's Landing
D. Asbury Park

3. What do the Kramdens name their adopted daughter?

4. On what date does Ralph first promise Alice that he is going to take her to a Broadway play?
A. August 5, 1942
B. October 27, 1946
C. September 30, 1948
D. November 9, 1944

5. In what month do the Kramdens get married?
A. March
B. July
C. September
D. December

6. Where do the Kramdens live when they first get married, and for how long?

7. In "TV or not TV," how long does Alice say that they have lived in their apartment without a stick of furniture being changed?
A. 9 years
B. 12 years
C. 14 years
D. 16 years

8. What is the Kramdens' telephone number in "The Babysitter"?

9. What was Ralph's pet name for Alice when they first got married?

10. What was Alice's pet name for Ralph when they first got married?

The Golfer

IN REAL LIFE, JACKIE GLEASON WAS AN AVID GOLFER. TOO BAD NONE OF HIS TALENTS RUBBED OFF ON RALPH. SEE IF YOU CAN GET A HOLE-IN-ONE BY ANSWERING ALL THESE QUESTIONS BASED ON THIS UNFORGETTABLE "CLASSIC 39" EPISODE DEVOTED TO GOLF.

1. What is the name of the bus company traffic manager that Ralph is supposed to play golf with?

2. At what golf course does the traffic manager usually play?

3. On what day of the week is Ralph's original golf date with the traffic manager, and to what day is it later changed?

4. At what time is Ralph supposed to tee off with the traffic manager?

5. According to Ed's golf book, what are the first three steps in setting up for a golf swing?

6. How does Ed Norton perform step three from the previous question?

7. What is written on the sign hanging in the bus company locker room?
A. No Profane Language   C. No Gambling
B. Employees Only   D. No Loitering

8. When the traffic manager has to cancel his golf date with Ralph, who takes his place?
A. Ed Norton   C. Mr. Douglas
B. Mr. Cassidy   D. Mr. Reilly

Name *that* Character II

CAN YOU IDENTIFY THE FOLLOWING HONEYMOONERS CHARACTERS BY THEIR FACES?

1. _____

2. _____

3. _____

4. _____

5. _____

6. _____

7. _____

8. _____

9. _____

Stand In for Murder

HERE'S A QUIZ BASED ON AN EPISODE IN WHICH JACKIE GLEASON PLAYS MORE THAN ONE ROLE. RALPH LOOKS JUST LIKE HARRY, A LOCAL MOB BOSS WHO'S ON A RIVAL MOB'S HIT LIST. THIS GIVES HARRY THE IDEA TO USE RALPH AS A CLAY PIGEON. USING THE 1954 VERSION OF THIS EPISODE AS YOUR GUIDE, TAKE A SHOT AT ANSWERING ALL OF THESE QUESTIONS CORRECTLY.

1. Harry the Mob Boss wants to leave the country. Where does he plan to go?
   A. Mexico
   B. Peru
   C. Cuba
   D. Colombia

2. Where does Nick the Mobster "discover" Ralph?
   A. in the bowling alley
   B. in the pool hall
   C. on Ralph's bus
   D. on the street

3. What type of business does Ralph think he is being made the district boss of?

4. Nick tells Ralph to use a secret knock when he gets to the Park Avenue apartment because they must be careful not to let in spies from which rival company?

5. How much is Ralph's weekly salary from his new "executive" position for the mob?
   A. $100.00
   B. $200.00
   C. $400.00
   D. $600.00

6. What is the name of the mob that wants to knock off Harry?
   A. North Side mob
   B. West Side mob
   C. Downtown mob
   D. Uptown mob

7. What type of car do the mobsters give to Ralph?
   A. Ford
   B. Nash
   C. Cadillac
   D. Mercedes

8. True or false: This is known as the episode without an ending.

9. What are the names of the two mobsters who visit Ralph at his apartment to offer him a job?
   A. Marty and Nick
   B. Frank and Marty
   C. Harry and Frank
   D. Frank and Nick

10. How is Ralph getting to Park Avenue on the first day of his new job?
    A. He's taking his new convertible.
    B. He's riding in his limousine.
    C. He's taking the bus.
    D. He's taking the train.

What Did You Call Me?

MATCH THE FOLLOWING EIGHT CHARACTERS WITH THE SATIRICAL OR PET NAME HE OR SHE WAS CALLED. TO ASSIST YOU, THE CORRESPONDING EPISODE NUMBER HAS BEEN PROVIDED. OBVIOUSLY, EACH OF THE EIGHT NAMES MAY BE USED MORE THAN ONCE.

RALPH   ED   RITA WEDEMEYER   WALLACE

ALICE   TRIXIE   BURT WEDEMEYER   JUDY CONNORS

1. _____: Sir Galahad (133)

2. _____: Madame Pompadour (133)

3. _____: Florence Nightingale (13)

4. _____: Lucius Bebe (64)

5. _____: Princess Grace (139)

6. _____: Kitten (126)

7. _____: Judy Garland (135)

8. _____: Atomic Passion (110)

9. _____: Dorothy Dix (112)

10. _____: Twinkles (126)

11. _____: Angel cake (110)

12. _____: Tubby (126)

13. _____: Bunny (105)

14. _____: Little speckled trout (63)

15. _____: Little sand crab (63)

16. _____: Buttercup (105)

17. _____: Happy Mildred (138)

18. _____: Henry VIII (84)

19. _____: Perry Como (82)

20. _____: J. Edgar Hoover (37)

21. _____: Pupi Campo (84)

22. _____: John J. Anthony (69)

23. _____: Diamond Jim (57)

24. _____: Matilda (77)

25. _____: Lady Godiva (88)

26. _____: Whispering Jack Smith (134)

What's Her Name?

CREDIT WAS NEVER GIVEN TO ANY ACTORS BESIDES THE KRAMDENS AND THE NORTONS AT THE END OF A HONEYMOONERS SKETCH. SEE HOW WELL YOU REALLY KNOW THE SHOW BY MATCHING THE HONEYMOONERS CHARACTER ON THE LEFT WITH THE NAME OF THE ACTRESS ON THE RIGHT WHO PLAYED THE PART.

1. Mrs. Gibson ("Classic 39")   Zamah Cunningham

2. Sally Gibson ("Game Called on Account of Marriage")   Betty Garde

3. Miss Lawrence ("The Adoption")   Gingr Jones

4. Mrs. Manicotti ("Classic 39")   Abby Lewis

5. Rita Wedemeyer ("Alice and the Blonde")   Ethel Owen

6. Nurse ("Ralph's Sweet Tooth")   Patti Pope Petrie

7. Thelma ("A Woman's Work Is Never Done")   Anne Seymour

8. Nurse ("Pal o' Mine")   Freda Rosen

Behind the Scenes

We all love Ralph, Alice, Ed, and Trixie, but let's not forget the other wisenheimers who helped make it all possible. See if you can unscramble the names of the following Honeymooners production team members.

1. CAKJ PLIBNIH — Executive Producer

2. AKJC REDUHL — Producer

3. LASTYEN SOPS — Assistant Producer

4. KAFNR NESTINTEAS — Director

5. RANVIM RAXM — Writer

6. ALRWTE NOSET — Writer

7. ETHBRER NIFN — Writer

8. J.A. LESRULS — Writer

9. RODNALE RENTS — Writer

10. YESDYN LKZAEIN — Writer

11. KCAJ OICSLEUEL — Announcer

12. NODRELA NOSDERAN — Film Editor

Food for Thought

IT'S TRUE THAT THE WAY TO A MAN'S HEART IS THROUGH HIS STOMACH, ESPECIALLY IN RALPH'S CASE. SEE IF YOU CAN DISH UP THE CORRECT ANSWERS BELOW BY MATCHING EACH OF THE FOODS FROM THE COLUMN ON THE LEFT WITH THE BEST DESCRIPTION FROM THE COLUMN ON THE RIGHT.

1. antipasto, a bowl of minestrone, spaghetti with meatballs, and an anchovy pizza

2. 4 cans frozen O.J., half a dozen fried eggs, a pound of bacon, a stack of toast, a steak, and 6 cups of coffee

3. hot tamales marinated in sour cream

4. 2 roast beef sandwiches, 2 hard-boiled eggs, 2 tomatoes, a piece of chocolate cake, and a Choosy Chews bar

5. pot roast, sauerkraut, and dumplings

6. pigs' knuckles, sauerkraut, and Neapolitan knockwurst

7. soup, roast chicken with stuffing, rice, salad, dessert, and coffee

8. strained prunes, farina, zwieback, and warm milk

9. pancakes, 5 eggs, bacon, and sausage

10. codfish cakes, macaroni and cheese, and fruit salad

11. corn beef hash, Spanish rice, and stewed prunes

12. wonton soup, spare ribs, egg roll, Sum Gum Chop Suey, butterfly shrimp, and fried rice

A. Being served at Eisenhower's inaugural dinner, according to Alice

B. Bus driver Fred Harvey's lunch

C. Dynamite Moran's breakfast

D. Ed Norton's leftover breakfast that was given to Ralph for supper

E. Ed Norton's lunch order at Pietro's and Coluchi's

F. The smell of foods that Ed Norton uses to determine the correct time

G. Meal that Alice prepared for dinner guests George and Henrietta

H. Ralph's breakfast when he has a cold

I. Ralph's favorite supper

J. Ralph's lunch order at Pietro's and Coluchi's

K. The average bus driver's hearty lunch, according to Ralph

L. The breakfast that Ralph couldn't eat because there was no gas or water in the apartment

M. Tuesday's canned-food dinner as planned by Alice in "The Next Champ"

13. Egg Foo Young and Moo Goo Gai Pan

14. 3 roast beef sandwiches, 2 hard-boiled eggs, soup, bread and butter, coffee, a few pieces of pie, and fruit

15. Fatchoomara's Matzaroni

16. Rofa cheese with chopped chives, anchovy paste, and clam juice

17. Yankee bean soup, meatloaf, French fries, peas and carrots, and a fruit cup

18. Cacciatore, and Linguini with Fatchoomara sauce

N. Type of cheese that Ralph requests for spaghetti and Ed goes to the store to buy

O. Types of pizza at the Racoon bowling team's victory feast

P. Wednesday's canned-food dinner as planned by Alice in "The Next Champ"

Q. What Joe Fensterblau wants for dinner at the Kramdens' apartment

R. What Ralph plans to order at the Royal Chinese Gardens

The Gift-Giver's Guide

WE ALL KNOW IT IS FAR GREATER TO GIVE THAN TO RECEIVE, BUT IS IT REALLY TRUE THAT IT'S THE THOUGHT THAT COUNTS? CHECK YOUR LIST TWICE AND SEE IF YOU CAN COME UP WITH THE GIFTS MENTIONED IN EACH OF THESE QUESTIONS.

1. Ed bought this for Trixie around tax day.

2. The Nortons gave this to Ralph for his birthday.

3. Alice went here to exchange a Christmas present.

4. Ed received this from his uncle when he was a kid (two words).

5. Ralph gave this to the building superintendent one Christmas.

6. Ed uses this as wrapping paper.

7. Trixie's gift to Ed that was used to plug a leak in the sewer.

8. For Christmas, Ed wanted to buy Ralph a book about _____.

9. Ralph gave this to the janitor for Christmas.

10. Ralph got this brass gift from his father.

11. Ralph got this antique gift from his grandfather.

12. Nick the Mobster gave this gas-guzzler to Ralph.

13. The Poor Soul gave this to Alice.

14. Reggie Van Gleason gave this kind of love potion to Alice.

15. Reggie Van Gleason gave this book to Trixie: *A Guide to the Second Best Hotels in* _____.

16. Reggie Van Gleason gave Ed a bicycle clip made of this material.

17. Ralph got this fur-lined gift from Alice.

18. Ralph bought this as a wedding gift for the boss's daughter.

19. Trixie gave these to Alice for her birthday (two words).

20. Type of Little Orphan Annie ring that Ed gave to Trixie for her birthday.

21. Mrs. Gibson gave this to Alice for her birthday.

22. Besides a night at the movies, Ed got this from Ralph and Alice for his birthday.

In the Hotel Business

In this memorable episode, Ralph and Ed thought they would strike it rich when they purchased a run-down hotel. They got the idea from Alice's brother, who was looking to buy it for himself but lacked the funds.

1. What is the name of the episode described above?

2. Which one of Alice's brothers asks to borrow money from Ralph for a down payment on the hotel?

3. Alice's brother has had some experience in the hotel business. What was his position at the Dixie Hotel?

4. What is odd about the way in which Alice's brother drinks coffee?

5. What is the name of the hotel that Ralph and Ed buy?

6. How much money do Ralph and Ed spend as a down payment on the hotel?

7. Where is the hotel located?

8. Match each character with his or her assigned job at the hotel.
   A. RALPH   chambermaid
   B. ALICE   bellhop
   C. ED   chef
   D. TRIXIE   manager

9. The hotel's first guest is a highway surveyor. Which room number is he given?

10. What is the highway surveyor's name?

11. Besides a pitcher of ice water, what else does the highway surveyor ask to be sent to his room?

12. We see Alice on the job at the hotel. What is written on her apron?

13. As it turns out, a new highway is being built that will pass _____ the hotel.
    A. in front of
    B. over
    C. behind
    D. under

14. Ralph implements an efficiency system based on bell taps. For the following, write in the number of bell taps that would signify each of the ensuing statements.
    A. _____ A guest wants ice water.
    B. _____ A guest's bags need to be picked up in the lobby.
    C. _____ The chef is wanted in the lobby.
    D. _____ A guest wants writing paper.
    E. _____ The chambermaid is wanted in the lobby.
    F. _____ A guest wants cigarettes.
    G. _____ The bellhop is wanted in the lobby.

Name that Character III

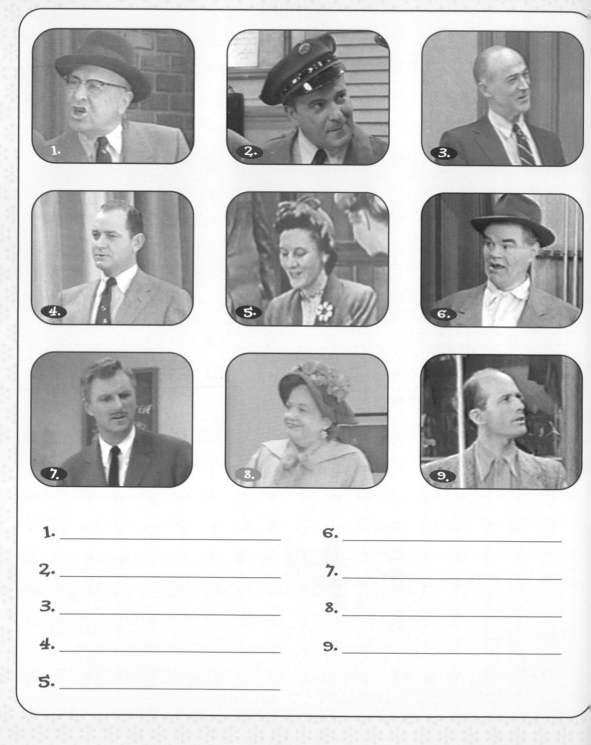

1. _____

2. _____

3. _____

4. _____

5. _____

6. _____

7. _____

8. _____

9. _____

What Did I Borrow?

FOR EACH OF THE FOLLOWING STATEMENTS, FIGURE OUT WHICH ITEM WAS BORROWED OR WHOM IT WAS BORROWED FROM BY UNSCRAMBLING THE SCRAMBLED WORD(S).

1. In "Ralph's Sweet Tooth," Trixie asks to borrow yellow SLOP HIHOSE from Alice.

2. In "Move Uptown," Trixie returns Alice's DEABEN BAGHDAD, which Trixie borrowed for her sister's wedding a long time ago.

3. Trixie borrowed GREEN ROATHES from Alice to try out her new Christmas present.

4. In "The Safety Award," Ed borrows Ralph's DECKAN-FIREHH.

5. Ralph borrowed a car from DRILLED FEMURE to get to City Hall.

6. In "Dial J for Janitor," Ed borrows a KNORMN CHEWEY from Ralph.

7. In "Dial J for Janitor," Alice borrows some PHADEHOE DRAWCE from Mrs. Manicotti.

8. In "New Year's Eve Party with the Dorseys," Ed borrows some CRUCHEMOMORER from Ralph for the lump on his head.

9. In "New Year's Eve Party with the Dorseys," Trixie offers to lend her CLERK BASDS to Alice for the party.

10. In "Norton Moves In," Ralph says he is going to return the OBLOGEN SWISH and GINSLOP HIFE that he borrowed from Norton.

11. Ralph and Ed first met ZARCAN SHOESCL when he asked to borrow a hammer from Ralph.

12. In "Guest Speaker," Trixie asks to borrow some DRACH BATKLE from Alice for Ed's pants.

13. In "Two Tickets to the Fight," Trixie borrows an ORC ARTWAR from Alice for Ed's supper.

14. In "Something Fishy," Ralph can't get the car started, but Alice fixes it with an IPHANRI that she borrows from Trixie.

YOU DON'T HAVE TO BE AN ACCOUNTANT TO ADD UP THE ANSWERS TO THESE NUMERICAL CHALLENGES, BUT A GOOD MEMORY FOR FIGURES JUST MIGHT HELP.

1. Fill in the blanks to complete the Racoon Lodge's marching song.

"In the _____ and in the _____
There's a mighty little _____.
For _____ there is no other.
When the _____ are all at stake
The Racoon will never _____.
We are proud to call him _____.
So with our noble _____ entwined
And a _____ strong of mind,
We'll have _____ that cannot melt.
In the forest, in the _____,
On the land or _____ _____,
We're _____ under the pelt.
Racoons, the _____ Racoons."

2. Who wrote the Racoons' marching song?

3. How much did the Racoons pay the songwriter for their marching song?

4. What is the name of the Racoons' bowling team?

5. Which of the following items is NOT in Ralph's bag of gags for the Racoon convention in Chicago?
A. chattering teeth   C. a hand buzzer
B. a dribble glass   D. an electric stick

6. The Racoons' drill team has had the honor of appearing on which popular television program?
A. *The Ed Sullivan Show*
B. *The Jackie Gleason Show*
C. *The Milton Berle Show*
D. *The Howdy Doody Show*

7. Which one of Ralph's brothers-in-law had his bachelor party at the Racoon Lodge?

8. What is the name of the finance company through which the Racoons purchased their pool table, television, phonograph, and piano?

9. What is the Racoons' slogan?

10. Between 1953 and 1955, how much money did the Racoons lose because of their annual dance?
A. $78.00   C. $208.00
B. $92.00   D. $378.00

Classic, Lost, or Late Model?

CATEGORIZE EACH OF THE FOLLOWING STATEMENTS AS HAVING FIRST OCCURRED IN A "LOST EPISODE," A "CLASSIC 39" EPISODE, OR AN EPISODE AIRED IN THE 1960S.

1. We see Ralph's boss Mr. Marshall for the first time.

2. The Racoons go to Chicago.

3. The Racoons go to Minneapolis.

4. The Racoons go to Miami.

5. Ed tries his luck at selling electric steam irons.

6. A Ralph Kramden look-alike is passing bad checks.

7. The Kramdens get evicted from their Chauncey Street apartment.

8. Ralph buys Alice a hairpin box made of 2,000 matchsticks glued together.

9. Ralph is running for assemblyman.

10. Alice and Trixie are kidnapped.

11. The IRS invites Ralph to clear something up on his tax return.

12. Ed is named Racoon of the Year at the lodge.

13. We meet Alice's millionaire uncle Howard.

14. Ralph has been transferred to the night shift and has trouble sleeping during the day.

15. Ralph is promoted to first assistant cashier to the assistant cashier.

16. Ralph and Ed shoot pool at Mr. Marshall's house.

17. Trixie gets a juice squeezer that's shaped like Napoleon as a Christmas gift from Ed.

18. Ralph and Ed enter a songwriting contest sponsored by movie star Washington Kenmore.

19. Ralph uses the rent money to renovate his apartment.

20. When the head Racoon asks Ralph to say a few words to his fellow brothers at the next meeting, Ralph takes it upon himself to write a whole speech.

Denizens of the Deep

HERE ARE A DOZEN STUMPERS BASED ON ED'S PLACE OF BUSINESS. ANSWER THE QUIZZES AND FILL IN THE QUOTES TO SHOW JUST HOW MUCH YOU KNOW ABOUT WHAT IT MEANS TO BE A SEWER SPELUNKER.

1. One of Ed's coworkers asks to borrow $2.00, and Ralph wonders why anybody would need money in the sewer. Which gambling game does Ed tell Ralph that the sewer workers play on payday?
A. Knights on Horseback C. Knuckle Knuckle
B. a floating crap game D. Underwater Poker

2. What does Ed get for his birthday from his coworkers that he can use at their annual spring Aquacade?
A. a surfboard   C. an inflatable vest
B. a shovel   D. a pair of swim fins

3. What game does Ed organize during Alphonse's birthday party in the sewer?
A. Knights on Horseback
B. Knuckle Knuckle
C. a three-legged swimming race
D. shovel tossing

4. Before Ed and Trixie were married, Ed wrote in a letter that since he has met Trixie, his sewer has become a what?
A. paradise   C. bundle of roses
B. home away from home D. tunnel of love

5. The sewer workers have a slogan about keeping a secret. What is it?
A. "A slip of the lip can sink a ship."
B. "Don't be a tattle tail."
C. "Keep your mouth shut."
D. "If you squeal, I'll drown you."

6. In "Mind Your Own Business," who does Ed think will get promoted in the sewer instead of himself?
A. Hagerty   C. Malone
B. Cassidy   D. Hofstetter

7. According to Ed, which theme song do they have in the sewer?
A. the Ajax theme song
B. the Drano theme song
C. the Bumblebee Tuna theme song
D. the Charmin theme song

8. According to Ed, how is a sewer worker similar to a brain surgeon?
A. They both wash their hands a lot.
B. They're both specialists.
C. They both like to pick your brain.
D. They're both experts on holes.

9. "If pizzas were manhole covers, the sewer would be a _____."

10. "As we say in the sewer, 'Here's _____ in your _____.'"

11. Ed says he has been working in the sewer for ten years. "If that don't qualify me as an expert on _____, I give up."

12. There's an old saying in the sewer: "_____ and _____ wait for no man."

93

Get the Facts Straight

WHEN YOU FIGURE IN ALL THE DIFFERENT SCRIPTWRITERS, VERY LITTLE REHEARSAL TIME, AND THE FACT THAT IT WAS A LIVE TELEVISION BROADCAST, IT'S NO WONDER THERE ARE SO MANY INCONSISTENCIES IN *The Honeymooners* CANON. SEE IF YOU CAN SPOT THE (IN)CORRECT CHOICE IN EACH OF THE FOLLOWING QUESTIONS.

1. Which of the following is NOT mentioned as Ralph's astrological sign?
A. Capricorn
B. Taurus
C. Pisces

2. Which of the following is NOT mentioned as Ed's astrological sign?
A. Libra
B. Sagittarius
C. Pisces

3. Which of the following is NOT mentioned as a way in which Ed got his job in the sewer?
A. He struck up a conversation with a sewer executive in a diner.
B. He chased a golf ball into an open manhole and met the foreman.
C. He took a civil service exam and his scores got mixed up with someone else's.

4. Which of the following is NOT mentioned as a way in which Ralph and Alice first met?
A. They met in a restaurant.
B. They met while working for the WPA.
C. They were introduced to each other by Phil Cuoco.
D. Ralph saw Alice walking home after school and offered to carry her books.

5. Which of the following is NOT mentioned as a way in which Ed and Trixie first met?
A. They sat next to each other in fifth grade.
B. They met at a burlesque house.
C. Ed got fresh with Trixie on the street.
D. They met at a dinner party.

6. Which of the following is NOT mentioned as a way in which Ralph and Ed first met?
A. They grew up together.
B. They met when the Kramdens moved to Chauncey Street and Ed invited them to dinner.
C. They met at a snooker parlor.
D. They met at the Racoon Lodge.

7. Which of the following is NOT mentioned as the name of Ralph's father?
A. Ed
B. Mike
C. Ralph

8. Which of the following is NOT mentioned as a Chauncey Street address for the Kramdens and Nortons?
A. 328 Chauncey Street
B. 358 Chauncey Street
C. 728 Chauncey Street
D. 758 Chauncey Street

The Icebox, the Sink, and the Bureau

THE MOST POPULAR SCENE ON *The Honeymooners* CONSISTED OF A FEW PIECES OF OUTDATED FURNITURE IN A COMBINATION KITCHEN/DINING ROOM. HERE'S A QUIZ BASED ON THREE ITEMS THAT DESERVE SPECIAL ATTENTION.

1. When Alice compares her apartment with Disneyland, what does she call the sink?
A. Frontierland   B. Tomorrowland
C. Adventureland   D. Fantasyland

2. When Alice compares her apartment with Disneyland, what does she call the icebox and stove?
A. Frontierland   B. Tomorrowland
C. Adventureland   D. Fantasyland

3. In "'Twas the Night Before Christmas," where do Ralph and Alice hide each other's gifts?
A. in the bureau   C. under the sink
B. under the bureau   D. under the icebox

4. When Alice opens the faucet it sounds like gunshots ringing through the pipes, so she asks a neighbor's child to turn a valve under the sink to see whether it fixes the problem. Who was the child?
A. Johnny Bennett   C. Eddie Hodges
B. Tommy Manicotti   D. Joey Garrity

5. In which of the following episodes is the candy bowl missing from atop the Kramdens' bureau?
A. "Ralph's Sweet Tooth"
B. "A Woman's Work Is Never Done"
C. "Champagne and Caviar"
D. "Alice and the Blonde"

6. Which parts of the icebox, sink, and bureau does Ralph use to make his outfit for the Racoons' costume contest?

7. Which of Alice's relatives once bought the Kramdens a new refrigerator as a gift?
A. her father   C. her uncle George
B. her brother Frank   D. her uncle Leo

8. Alice tells Ralph that she's sick of looking at "that icebox, that stove, that sink, and these four walls." What does she want to look at instead?

9. In "Teamwork Beat the Clock," Ralph has a bunch of balloons in the kitchen sink. What does Ed throw in the sink that pops the balloons?

10. In which of the following episodes do the Kramdens have a radio on top of the icebox?
A. "The Songwriters"
B. "Mama Loves Mambo"
C. "Good Night Sweet Prince"
D. "Dinner Guests"

The Flab Four

ALTHOUGH *The Honeymooners* SAW MANY CHARACTERS WALK ACROSS ITS STAGE OVER THE YEARS, THE FOUR CHARACTERS WHO MADE THE SHOW AND WON ALL OUR HEARTS FOREVER WERE RALPH, ALICE, ED, AND TRIXIE. SEE HOW MUCH YOU KNOW ABOUT THE QUERULOUS QUARTET.

Ralph

1. Ralph's bus has been held up six times. No money was taken the first five times, but what did the robbers get the last time?

2. In one episode, we see Ralph take a magazine out of the garbage and start to read it. Who was on the cover of the magazine?

3. Ralph attended a Racoons' costume party as a man from space. What did the contest judges think Ralph was dressed as?

4. Ralph has wanted to be something in the sports world all his life. He wanted to play _____, but he was too slow. He wanted to play _____, but he was too short. He wanted to be a _____, but he was a little too heavy.

5. True or false: Ralph had to get his mother's permission before getting married.

Alice

1. Where did Alice learn shorthand and typing?

2. Ralph boasts to Alice that he can do just as good on a quiz show as the twelve-year-old kid who answered the $16,000.00 question. What word does Alice ask Ralph to spell?

3. When Alice was learning to do the mambo, the lesson ran late and she didn't have time to make a hot meal for Ralph. What did she decide to prepare for him?

4. What does Alice use to make the halo for her angel costume in "Halloween Party"?

5. Who did Alice hire for musical diversion when Ralph was on the entertainment committee for the bus driver's ball?

Ed

1. When Ed lied about being the owner of a horse named Cigar Box, what did he say his own name was?

2. In "The Loudspeaker," from where does Ed say that he got his vest?

3. When Ed was in the Navy, he frequently suffered from bad headaches. What caused them?

4. In "Expectant Fathers," we see Ed juggling three fruits. What kind of fruits are they?

5. What did Ed lose in the sourball jar at George Winters' apartment?

Trixie

1. Trixie once bought a mystery can without a label. What was in the can?

2. What did Alice borrow from Trixie that contained a love letter written by Ed before he and Trixie were married?

3. Which one of Trixie's showbiz friends came to visit on Christmas Eve in 1953?

4. In which episode does Trixie make Ed wear her dress so that she can fix the hem?

5. In "Oh My Aching Back," Trixie spends the night at a relative's house. Whose house does she go to?

Name that Character IV

1. _____   6. _____

2. _____   7. _____

3. _____   8. _____

4. _____   9. _____

5. _____

Anniversary Quiz

HERE'S A QUIZ BASED ON AN ANNUAL EVENT THAT RALPH SEEMS TO HAVE A HARD TIME REMEMBERING. SEE HOW WELL YOU CAN REMEMBER THE ANSWERS TO THESE TRICKY QUESTIONS.

1. In "Double Anniversary," Alice is having a surprise anniversary party for Ralph. Where is the party taking place?
   A. in the Kramdens' apartment
   B. in the Nortons' apartment
   C. at the Kit Kat Club
   D. at the Hong Kong Gardens

2. In "Double Anniversary," where is Ralph planning to take Alice for their anniversary?
   A. the movies
   B. the Hong Kong Gardens
   C. the Kit Kat Club
   D. the Royal Chinese Gardens

3. In the 1977 special "The Second Honeymoon," which anniversary are the Kramdens celebrating?
   A. their 20th   C. their 30th
   B. their 25th   D. their 35th

4. Ralph and Alice once celebrated their wedding anniversary with a second ceremony. Where did the ceremony take place?
   A. at the Racoon Lodge
   B. at the Kit Kat Club
   C. at Niagara Falls
   D. at the Hong Kong Gardens

5. In "Anniversary Gift," Alice gives Ralph money so he can buy himself an anniversary present. What is he supposed to spend the money on?
   A. a bowling ball   C. the Racoons' convention
   B. a pool cue   D. a suede coat

6. In "Anniversary Gift," what does Alice think that Ralph bought her for their anniversary?
   A. an orange juice maker
   B. a box for hairpins
   C. a dress
   D. curtains for the kitchen

7. In "Anniversary Gift," who buys Alice the same gift that Ralph bought for their anniversary?
   A. Mrs. Stevens   C. Mrs. Manicotti
   B. Trixie   D. Mrs. Gibson

8. Episodes in which the Kramdens are celebrating a wedding anniversary have aired in several different months. Which of the following months has never been host to an original broadcast of a Kramdens' anniversary episode?
   A. January   C. October
   B. February   D. November

9. The month in which the Kramdens celebrate their wedding anniversary has been mentioned only once. Which month was it?
   A. March   C. September
   B. April   D. December

10. In "Double Anniversary," what song does Ralph request the band play when he and Alice enter the establishment?
    A. "Happy Anniversary"
    B. "You're My Greatest Love"
    C. "Anniversary Waltz"
    D. "Melancholy Serenade"

Tax Day

1. While comparing their taxes, Ralph and Norton realize that they pay $90.00 in rent between them. They decide to share an apartment in Flushing to save money. What is their new address?

2. In "Income Tax Time," how much does Ralph estimate that he owes the government?
   A. $5.00   C. $15.00
   B. $10.00   D. $20.00

3. In "The Worry Wart," how much does Ralph expect back from the IRS?
   A. $36.00   C. $53.00
   B. $42.00   D. $62.00

4. In "The Worry Wart," why does the IRS want to see Ralph?

5. In "Income Tax," what does Ralph do with the money that he was saving to buy a bowling ball?

6. In "The Worry Wart," what does Ed Norton tell the IRS employee that he didn't claim on his taxes?

7. In "The Worry Wart," which of the following items does Ralph not tell the IRS employee about?
   A. His gambling winnings
   B. The horse with the clock in its stomach
   C. Winning a three-legged race
   D. A skinny chicken he got as a bonus

Norton, Come on Down...

HIS WIFE TRIXIE CALLS HIM HER HUSBAND; HIS BEST FRIEND RALPH CALLS HIM A MENTAL CASE. THIS QUIZ TESTS YOUR KNOWLEDGE ABOUT EVERYONE'S FAVORITE "ENGINEER IN SUBTERRANEAN SANITATION."

1. When is Ed Norton's birthday?

2. Which branch of the military did Ed serve in?

3. What does the "L" in Edward L. Norton stand for?

4. Ed is proud of the fact that he once kept a yo-yo going for how many consecutive hours?

5. What is the name of the stickball team that Ed coaches?

6. What is the name of the best dog Ed Norton ever had?

7. In "Mind Your Own Business," how many prospects did Ed visit to try and sell irons?

8. In "The Sleepwalker," which magazine does Ed read before going to sleep?
A. *Mickey Mouse*
B. *Esquire*
C. *Cosmo*
D. *Capt. Video Ranger's Handbook*

9. What company makes the broken watch that Ed wears in "Unconventional Behavior"?

10. What material is Ed's vest made of?
A. Cotton   C. Polyester
B. Silk   D. Cashmere

The NYC Dept. of Subterranean Sanitation

HOW MUCH DO YOU KNOW ABOUT NORTON'S UNDERGROUND HOME AWAY FROM HOME? TRY YOUR HAND AT ANSWERING THESE CHALLENGING QUESTIONS ABOUT THE DENIZENS OF THE DEEP.

1. What does Sewer Ordinance 408-2, section 5, paragraph B, state?

2. On what street is the sewer explosion that lands Ed Norton in the hospital?

3. To what hospital is Ed taken after a manhole cover lands on his head, and what is his room number?

4. In "Pal o' Mine," who gives Ed his start in the sewer, and what is his nickname?

5. What is the top position one can hold in the Department of Sewers?

6. Fill in the blanks to complete the following sewer saying:

"When the _____ of _____
   turn against you,
And the _____ upsets your boat,
Don't waste those tears on what
   might have been,
Just lay on your _____ and _____."

All About Pets

THROUGH THE YEARS, MANY PETS SAW THEIR WAY INTO THE SCRIPT, AND SOME EVEN MADE IT ONSTAGE. SEE HOW MUCH YOU KNOW ABOUT SOME OF THE UNSUNG HONEYMOONERS PETS.

1. What is the name of the bird that Ralph inherits from Mrs. Monahan?
A. Fortune
B. Treasure
C. Polly
D. Squawky

2. Where does Ed Norton lose the best dog he ever had?

3. In "Boxtop Kid," Ralph wins a dog in a contest. What is the name of the dog food company he gets it from?

4. What does Ralph get from his boss for doing a great job on the Christmas play in "The Honeymooners Christmas Carol"?

5. What kind of dog does Alice's mother have, and what is its name?

6. In "A Dog's Life," what kind of dog does Alice get?
A. Poodle
B. Cocker spaniel
C. Cocker poodle
D. Beagle hound

7. In "A Dog's Life," how many dogs does Ralph leave the pound with?

I Have a Big Mouth

WHETHER HE'S LYING, BRAGGING, OR GIVING (USUALLY BAD) ADVICE, RALPH IS ALWAYS GETTING HIMSELF IN TROUBLE BY SHOOTING OFF HIS BIG FAT MOUTH. TEST YOUR KNOWLEDGE OF RALPH'S LOUDMOUTH MISFORTUNES WITH THE FOLLOWING TWELVE STUMPERS.

1. Ralph tells George the traffic manager that Alice wants to set him up with a monster, but the "monster" turns out to be George's

   _____.

   A. sister   C. fiancée
   B. girlfriend D. neighbor

2. Ralph tries to get rid of a houseguest by staging a phony backache, but the guest stays on to nurse Ralph back to health. Who is the guest?
   A. Uncle Leo   C. Alice's mother
   B. Aunt Ethel   D. Alice's sister Agnes

3. Ralph tells Ed that he knows a famous celebrity, and Ed tells the Racoons. Now they want Ralph to get the celebrity to attend the Racoons' annual dance. Who is the celebrity?

4. Ralph tells a fellow Racoon about a great vacuum cleaner that he bought for $4.95, and that admission ends up costing Ralph the election for convention manager. Which Racoon double-crosses Ralph because of the vacuum?

5. Ralph thinks he's been fired, so he writes a nasty letter to his boss, but later finds out that he was promoted. Who mails the letter?
   A. Ralph
   B. Ed
   C. Alice
   D. the bowling alley custodian

6. Ralph thinks that Alice wants to increase his life insurance, so when a doctor comes to examine Ralph, he makes believe he's a drunk. Where was the doctor really from?

7. Bill Davis lies to Ralph about owning a factory in Akron. What does Bill really do for a living?

8. Ralph gives some bad advice to Ed that gets him fired from his job in the sewer. What job does Ed try his luck at, but doesn't do very well?

9. Ralph shoots off his big mouth by picking on a little guy at the pool hall, and now he is faced with a fight against a big bully. What is the bully's name?

10. Ed has two tickets to the fights, so Ralph fakes a backache to get out of having to stay home for dinner with Alice's uncle. Ed is taken in by the act and offers the ticket to Alice's uncle, who gladly accepts. What is the uncle's name, and where does he live?

11. Ralph gives some bad marital advice to his future brother-in-law, which results in the couple's having a big fight right after the wedding. What are the newlyweds' names?

12. Ralph fakes an illness so that he doesn't have to work on New Year's Eve, but then he runs into his boss and almost loses his job. Where does Ralph run into Mr. Marshall?

Boys' Night Out

BETWEEN GOING BOWLING, SHOOTING POOL, AND ATTENDING LODGE MEETINGS IT'S NO WONDER RALPH IS ALWAYS BROKE—AND ALICE IS ALWAYS COMPLAINING THAT SHE NEVER GOES OUT. HERE ARE TEN QUESTIONS BASED ON RALPH AND ED'S OUTINGS.

1. When Ralph goes to the pool hall without Ed in "The Little Man Who Wasn't There," who does he shoot pool with?
   A. Frank
   B. Joe
   C. Harry
   D. Stanley

2. In "Kramden vs. Norton," who accompanies Ralph to the pool hall?

3. When Alice and Trixie play pool against each other in a bet between Ralph and Ed, which of the wives breaks the balls?

4. Ralph and Ed once lost in a game of pool against Trixie and _____.
   A. Alice
   B. Trixie's father
   C. Trixie's mother
   D. Ed's sister

5. Ralph tied the house record for sinking the most consecutive balls at the pool hall, but missed the tiebreaker because of Ed. How many balls did Ralph sink?
   A. eight
   B. thirteen
   C. seventeen
   D. twenty-two

6. According to Ralph in "Trapped," when Ralph and Ed shoot pool, how much do they usually wager against each other?
   A. a penny a ball
   B. 2 cents a ball
   C. a nickel a ball
   D. a crack over the knuckles a ball

7. Which rival team did the Racoons beat in the bowling championship that earned Ralph an MVP trophy?
   A. Secaucus
   C. Flushing
   B. Bushwick
   D. Bayonne

8. In "Something Fishy," Ralph and Ed are playing Ping-Pong against each other at the lodge. What's the score and how much money is at stake?

9. Whose car does Ralph borrow to get to the pier for the Racoons' fishing trip in "Something Fishy"?

10. Where were Ralph and Ed returning from when they ran into Ralph's old classmate Herman Gruber?
    A. the bowling alley
    B. the pool hall
    C. the Racoon Lodge
    D. the Kit Kat Club

Hey There Ralphie Boy!

HERE'S A CHANCE TO SEE HOW MUCH YOU REALLY KNOW ABOUT THE MAN WHO "BRIVES A DUS" FOR A LIVING.

1. Ralph's age was mentioned only once. How old was he at the time?
A. 39   C. 46
B. 42   D. 51

2. What is the name of the grade school that Ralph attended?

3. What is the highest grade that Ralph completed in school?

4. Name the three game shows that Ralph has been on.

5. Ralph has appeared on TV in three commercials. What products was he advertising?

6. In how many of the "Classic 39" episodes does Ralph not wear his bus driver's uniform?
A. none   C. 3
B. 1   D. 6

7. How tall is Ralph?

8. What is Ralph's neck size?

9. What is Ralph's waist size?
A. 42 inches   C. 52 inches
B. 47 inches   D. 57 inches

10. What is Ralph's Social Security number? (Back then, they were only 7 numbers long.)
A. 050-48-13   C. 105-28-42
B. 050-62-49   D. 105-36-22

11. What is Ralph's blood type?

12. In "Letter to the Boss," what time does Ralph say he wakes up to go to work every morning?
A. 5 A.M.   C. 7 A.M.
B. 6 A.M.   D. 8 A.M.

13. In "A Weighty Problem," how much does Ralph weigh?

Election Day

1. In "Forgot to Register," who are the two candidates running against each other in the local election?

2. In "Forgot to Register," Ralph and Norton campaign for which candidate?

3. In "Forgot to Register," which candidate is Alice going to vote for?

4. In "The Deciding Vote," who is Ralph running against in the Racoon election for Convention Manager?
A. Jerry Shor   C. Frank McGillicuddy
B. Charlie Sullivan   D. Joe Rumsey

5. In "The People's Choice," what are the names of the two gentlemen who ask Ralph to run for assemblyman?

6. In "Two Men on a Horse," what is the campaign promise that wins Ralph the Racoon election?

Unconventional Behavior

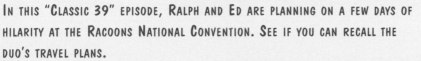

In this "Classic 39" episode, Ralph and Ed are planning on a few days of hilarity at the Racoons National Convention. See if you can recall the duo's travel plans.

1. Who is bringing each of the following items to the convention, Ralph or Ed?
   A. Trick camera
   B. Rubber marshmallow
   C. Cherry bombs
   D. Fake box of candy
   E. Bulging eyes
   F. Hand buzzer
   G. Trick handcuffs
   H. Paper bags

2. Oops, wrong train! Where is their train really headed?

3. What time does their train leave the station?

4. Where is the convention taking place?

5. For how many days do Ralph and Ed plan on attending the convention?

6. What is Ralph and Ed's berth number on the train?

7. Which of the following does Ed complain that he can't sleep on?
   A. his side
   B. his back
   C. his stomach

8. According to Ed, how fast does the aroma of Egg Foo Young rise?

Weight Watcher

HERE'S A QUIZ BASED ON TWO VERY SIMILAR EPISODES: "RALPH'S DIET" AND "A WEIGHTY PROBLEM." IN FACT, THE LATTER IS AN "EXPANDED" VERSION OF THE FORMER.

1. With Norton's help, Ralph measures himself to be six feet tall. The bus company guidelines say he can weigh up to 250 pounds for this height. Is Ralph overweight or underweight, and by how much?

2. Ralph finds out that he is really only 5'11". Why is he an inch shorter than the first time he was measured?
A. Norton made a mistake.
B. Ralph was wearing his shoes.
C. Ralph was wearing a hat.
D. An inch was missing off the first measuring tape.

3. Now at 5'11", Ralph weighs more than the maximum listed in the bus company guidelines. How much weight does he have to lose within the next week so that he can pass the physical?
A. four pounds
B. six pounds
C. eight pounds
D. ten pounds

4. Which neighbor is having a surprise birthday party for her husband in "A Weighty Problem"?
A. Mrs. Stevens   C. Mrs. Rafferty
B. Mrs. Manicotti   D. Mrs. Fogarty

5. Which neighbor is having a surprise birthday party for her husband in "Ralph's Diet"?
A. Mrs. Stevens   C. Mrs. Rafferty
B. Mrs. Manicotti   D. Mrs. Fogarty

6. Which food item does the neighbor ask Alice to hide in "A Weighty Problem" that was not hidden in "Ralph's Diet"?
A. ham   C. cake
B. turkey   D. ice cream

7. What does Ralph's supper consist of in "A Weighty Problem"?
A. half a grapefruit and a poached egg
B. one hard-boiled egg, two stalks of celery, and an apple
C. raw vegetable salad
D. one celery stick and a glass of sauerkraut juice

8. What does Ralph's supper consist of in "Ralph's Diet"?
A. half a grapefruit and a poached egg
B. one hard-boiled egg, two stalks of celery, and an apple
C. raw vegetable salad
D. one celery stick and a glass of sauerkraut juice

9. What does Norton borrow from a secondhand store to help Ralph lose weight in "A Weighty Problem"?

10. In both episodes, Ralph goes crazy when he sees the food. In which episode does he eat only the cake, not any of the meat?

Fred's Landing

1. Ralph and Ed want to spend their vacation fishing at Fred's Landing. Where do the wives want to go?

2. How long is Ralph and Ed's vacation?

3. What hotel does Alice recommend the two couples stay in while on vacation?

4. In which state is Fred's Landing located?
A. New York
B. New Jersey
C. Connecticut
D. Pennsylvania

5. When Ed was a kid he would go fishing from a bridge every night, but he never caught anything. One night he fished until the sun came up and found out the problem. Why didn't Ed catch any fish?

6. Who loans his car to Ralph for the trip to Fred's Landing?

7. Which large prop do Ralph and Ed carry on to the set in the 1953 version of this episode?
A. a canoe
B. a barbecue grill
C. a tent
D. a bear suit

8. How long do the Kramdens and Nortons end up staying at Fred's Landing?

9. Who is planning on wearing a bear suit to scare the wives into leaving Fred's Landing?

10. When the car that Ralph borrowed breaks down, a passerby offers to help fix it. What does he say is wrong with the car?
A. The radiator needs water.
B. There's no gas in the tank.
C. The spark plugs aren't connected to the distributor.
D. The starter wires are loose.

11. How many fish do Ralph and Ed manage to catch and keep the whole time they're at Fred's Landing?

12. Fill in the blanks to complete Ralph's description of Fred's Landing.
"A vacationer's _____ nestled in the foothills of the _____ Mountains, overlooking Lake _____."

Name That Tune

1. What is the name of *The Honeymooners* theme song?

2. In "Young at Heart," what song does Ed play on the phonograph to teach Ralph how to dance?

3. In "Mama Loves Mambo," what song does Carlos play on the phonograph, and who is the artist?

4. What song does Ed Norton have to warm up with before playing the piano?

5. According to Ralph in *"The $99,000 Answer,"* each of the songs on the left belongs with which of the composers on the right?

A. "Don't Fence Me In"	Johnny Mercer and Richard Whiting
B. "Shuffle Off to Buffalo"	Cole Porter
C. "Just Too Marvelous for Words"	Ernesto Dequista
D. "Take Me Back to Sorrento"	Warren-Dubin

6. Which one of the artists in the previous question does not really exist?

"Classic 39" Classic Lines

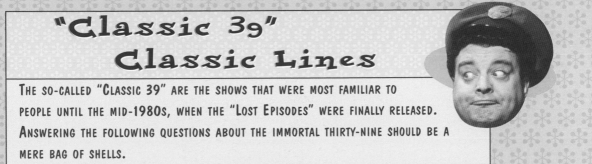

THE SO-CALLED "CLASSIC 39" ARE THE SHOWS THAT WERE MOST FAMILIAR TO PEOPLE UNTIL THE MID-1980S, WHEN THE "LOST EPISODES" WERE FINALLY RELEASED. ANSWERING THE FOLLOWING QUESTIONS ABOUT THE IMMORTAL THIRTY-NINE SHOULD BE A MERE BAG OF SHELLS.

1. How many episodes end with some variation of "Baby, you're the greatest"?
A. 1   B. 4   C. 7   D. 9

2. In how many episodes does Ralph say "Bang, Zoom"?
A. 1   B. 4   C. 7   D. 9

3. In how many episodes does Ralph say, "One of these days, pow! Right in the kisser!"?
A. 1   B. 4   C. 7   D. 9

4. In how many episodes does Ralph say, "a mere bag of shells"?
A. 1   B. 4   C. 7   D. 9

5. Complete the following line from Ed's dialogue in the advertisement for a handy kitchen gadget: "Now ol' chef of the future, I will admit it can sharpen a knife better. But, can it _____ __ _____?"

Read All About It

FOR CENTURIES, THE PRINTED MEDIA HAVE BEEN A MAJOR SOURCE OF INFORMATION AND ENTERTAINMENT FOR EVERYONE, EVEN TV FAMILIES LIKE THE KRAMDENS AND NORTONS. SEE HOW LITERATE YOU ARE WHEN IT COMES TO THE PRINTED MATTER OF HONEYMOONERS-ERA BENSONHURST.

1. Alice read in a magazine that 50 percent of the pain a person feels is _____.

2. While trying to get his mind off of his appointment with the IRS, Ralph read a story in the newspaper about a new highway in Tibet. Where does this highway go?
A. Burma
B. India
C. Pakistan
D. Mongolia

3. In "The Babysitter," which magazine does Ed pick up while waiting for Ralph to get a shave at the barbershop?
A. *Esquire*
B. *Cosmopolitan*
C. *Mickey Mouse*
D. *Look*

4. In which magazine did Alice read about scientists isolating the cold germ?
A. *Scientific American*
B. *Redbook*
C. *Cosmopolitan*
D. *Good Housekeeping*

5. Alice got a recipe for raw vegetable salad out of a movie magazine. Which actor eats it, according to Alice?
A. Gene Kelly
B. Fred Astaire
C. Robert Taylor
D. John Wayne

6. Alice read an article in a movie magazine that was written by the recently divorced Arline Judge. What was the title of the article?
A. "How to Hold a Husband"
B. "My Eight Divorces"
C. "How to Commit Marriage"
D. "My Dream Wedding"

7. In "Champagne and Caviar," Ralph pulls a magazine out of the garbage can and sits down to read it. Which magazine is it?
A. *Esquire*
B. *Cosmopolitan*
C. *TV Magazine*
D. *Look*

8. Which magazine did a three-page article on Ralph's safety record with the bus company?
A. *Universal Magazine*
B. *Look*
C. *Family Circle*
D. *Time*

9. In "Letter to the Boss," after thinking he has been fired from the bus company, Ralph checks the newspaper for a new job. What is wrong with all the jobs he sees in the newspaper?
A. They're too far from home.
B. They don't pay enough.
C. They're all for women.
D. They require a higher education.

10. What is the name of the inquisitive photographer who published Ralph's statements about being king of his castle?
A. Tom
B. Dick
C. Charlie
D. George

Show and Tell

For all their meager resources, Ralph and the gang certainly get into some interesting jams and meet some interesting people. Based on these pictures, see if you can answer the corresponding questions.

1. Who is Ralph dancing with?

2. Why is Ralph wearing a blindfold?

3. What does Ralph have on his head?

4. What is Ralph dressed as?

5. What is on Ralph's face?

6. What is wrong with Ralph?

7. From where did Ralph and Alice just return?

8. Who is in this picture?

9. Specifically, what is on Alice's face?

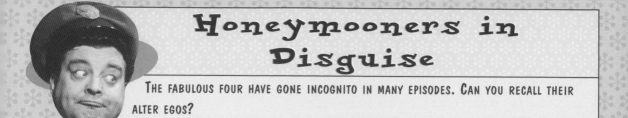

Honeymooners in Disguise

THE FABULOUS FOUR HAVE GONE INCOGNITO IN MANY EPISODES. CAN YOU RECALL THEIR ALTER EGOS?

1. In "Vacation at Fred's Landing," what is Ralph going to dress as in order to scare the wives?

2. In "Petticoat Jungle," what is Ed going to dress as in order to scare the wives?

3. In "The Man From Space," Ed dresses as the person who he thinks designed the sewers of Paris. What is his name?

4. In "The Man From Space," what costume does Ralph want to rent?

5. In "The Man From Space," what does Trixie go to the costume party dressed as?

6. In "The Man From Space," what does Alice go to the costume party dressed as?

7. Match the costume with the person who wears it in "Halloween Party."

A. Clara Bow   Ralph
B. Sailor   Alice
C. Angel   Ed
D. Zulu Chief   Trixie

8. In "Halloween Party," Ralph doesn't like his original costume, so he tears up his tuxedo and dresses up as what?

All About Trixie

1. What is Trixie's real name?

    A. Patricia   B. Tracy

    C. Thelma   D. Agnes

2. When is Trixie's birthday?

3. True or False: Trixie used to be a burlesque dancer.

4. Which branch of the military did Trixie serve in?

    A. Army   B. Navy

    C. Air Force D. Marines

5. In the episode called "Songs and Witty Sayings," Ed tells Ralph that Trixie was the original actress in a famous sketch. Unscramble the name of that sketch:

    GELLOFO ETSERT

6. In which episode do we find out that Trixie played in vaudeville?

7. True or False: Trixie has a tattoo.

8. In which episode from the 1950s does Trixie rehearse lines for a play she is in?

9. In which episode does Trixie wear an imitation dyed rabbit fur coat (although the television audience never actually sees it)?

117

Complete the Title

1. "The Next _____"

2. "_____ and _____ Together"

3. "_____ Hats"

4. "_____ Kid"

5. "_____ _____ Through _____"

6. "_____ and _____ Sayings"

7. "_____ For Sale"

8. "_____ over _____"

9. "_____ Plays _____"

10. "Funny _____"

11. "A _____ Problem"

12. "_____ Called on _____ of _____"

13. "Pardon My _____"

14. "Something _____"

15. "My Fair _____"

16. "The _____ in the _____ _____"

17. "_____ _____ But"

18. "_____ Loves _____"

19. "Two _____ on a _____"

20. "The Great _____ _____"

21. "_____ _____ Sweet _____"

22. "_____ Man with a _____"

23. "Good Bye _____ _____"

24. "The _____ _____ Who _____ There"

25. "Two _____ to the _____"

26. "A _____ of _____ and _____"

27. "_____ Moves _____"

28. "A _____ _____ Is Never _____"

29. "_____ of the Thing"

30. "Oh My _____ _____"

Hare-Brained Schemes

FROM HOUSEHOLD APPLIANCES TO PURCHASING REAL ESTATE, RALPH AND ED'S MONEY-MAKING SCHEMES ALWAYS RAISED A LOT OF LAUGHS, BUT NO MONEY. SEE IF YOU CAN FILL IN THE BLANKS TO COMPLETE THE NAMES OF SOME OF THEIR PRICELESS HARE-BRAINED VENTURES.

1. Pills that turn water into _ _ _ _ _ _ _ _ _

2. _ _ _ _ gland vitamins

3. _ _ _ _ _ _ _ shoehorns

4. _ _ _ _ _ _ _ _ _ _ _ _ in Asbury Park

5. _ _ _ _ - _ _ - _ _ _ - _ _ _ _ shoe polish

6. Managing a _ _ _ _ _

7. Buying a hotel in _ _ _ _ _ _ _ _ _

8. _ _ - _ _ _ pizza

9. Digging for _ _ _ _ _ _ _ _ _ _ _'s treasure on Long Island

10. Handy _ _ _ _ _ _ _ _ _ Helper tool

11. _ _ _ _ _ _ _ _ Delicious _ _ _ _ _ _ _ Appetizer

12. Miracle _ _ _ _ restorer

The Trip to Europe

THE SHIP HAS FINALLY COME IN FOR THE KRAMDENS AND THE NORTONS, AND NOW THEY'RE OFF TO EUROPE! REFERRING TO SOME OF THE SELDOM-SEEN SKETCHES FROM THE 1960S, SEE HOW WELL YOU CAN REMEMBER THESE CLASSIC COLOR EPISODES.

1. Complete the following slogan that wins Ralph a trip to Europe from the Flakey Wakey cereal company: "Flakey Wakeys add to the _____, but take away from your _____ _____ _____."

2. What is the Kramdens' and Nortons' first stop on their trip to Europe?

3. What is the name of the boy that Alice asks to be their guide in Rome?

4. Ralph and Ed go hunting while on a safari. What animal does each of them kill?

5. Where is the haunted Kramden castle in which Ralph and Ed spend the night?

6. Which of the following is not a stop on the trip to Europe?
A. Madrid, Spain
B. London, England
C. Athens, Greece
D. Berlin, Germany

7. What are the names of the couple that blackmail Ralph with a phony picture?

All About the Racoons

ACCORDING TO RALPH, THE RACOONS ARE A VERY WORTHWHILE ORGANIZATION. HERE ARE A FEW QUESTIONS TO TEST YOUR KNOWLEDGE ABOUT THIS MODEL SOCIAL INSTITUTION.

1. Which of the following is not mentioned as an official title for the Racoons?
A. The International Order of Racoons
B. The International Order of Friendly Racoons
C. The International Order of Friendly Sons of the Racoons
D. The International Order of Loyal Racoons

2. In what year was the Racoon Lodge established?
A. 1895   C. 1938
B. 1907   D. 1951

3. What is the highest title that can be held by a Racoon?
A. Grand Imperial Mystic Ruler of All Racoondom
B. Almighty Ruler of the International Order of the Racoons
C. President at Arms
D. Grand High Exalted Mystic Ruler

4. Complete the Racoons' toast:
"_____ to _____, _____ to _____, watch out below, here she comes!"

5. Which of the following titles has Ralph held at the Racoon Lodge? Select all that apply.
A. Chairman of the dance committee
B. Racoon of the Year
C. Secretary
D. Treasurer
E. Sergeant at Arms
F. President

6. Which of the following titles has Ed Norton held at the Racoon Lodge? Select all that apply.
A. Chairman of the dance committee
B. Racoon of the Year
C. Secretary
D. Treasurer
E. Sergeant at Arms
F. President

7. Whose father had the honor of being a thirteen-tail Racoon?

Get Out!!!

RALPH'S TEMPER IS SOMETIMES SHORTER THAN NORTON'S ATTENTION SPAN. USING THE "CLASSIC 39" AS YOUR GUIDE, SEE IF YOU CAN FIGURE OUT HOW MANY TIMES RALPH HAS THROWN EACH OF THE FOLLOWING PEOPLE OUT OF HIS APARTMENT.

1. ALICE KRAMDEN

2. ED NORTON

3. TRIXIE NORTON

4. MRS. MANICOTTI

5. MR. MANICOTTI

6. TONY AMICO

7. CARLOS SANCHEZ

8. JIM MCKEEVER

9. MRS. GIBSON

10. MRS. STEVENS

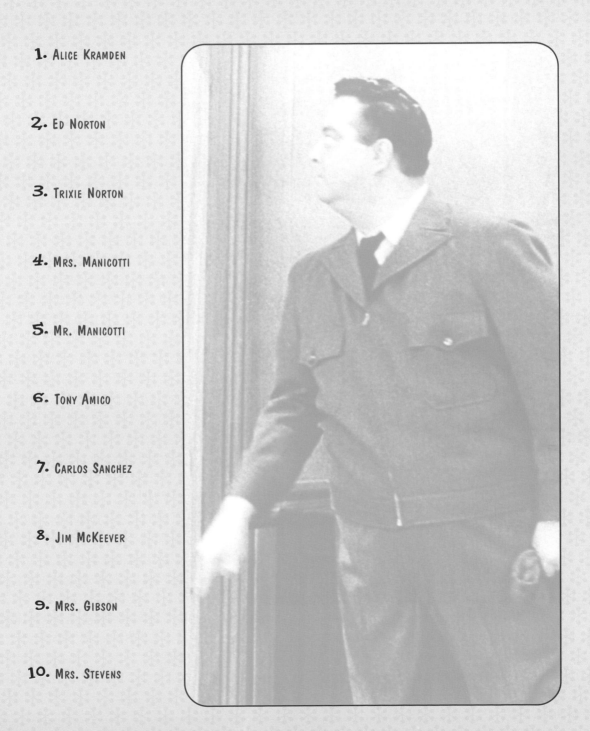

Potluck Final Exam

1. What color is the suit that Alice gives to charity in "The Man in the Blue Suit"?

2. From what year is the bottle of champagne that Ralph buys in "Champagne and Caviar"?
A. 1939   C. 1951
B. 1946   D. 1953

3. Who claimed that his grandfather invented the first television in 1773, but it didn't work because there was no electricity back then?

4. True or false: Trixie once had a bit part in a John Boles movie.

5. True or false: Alice's brother Leo was once in a Broadway show called *George White's Scandals*.

6. The bus company sent Ralph to a psychiatrist because several passengers complained about his attitude. What hobby did the psychiatrist suggest that Ralph take up to try to calm his nerves?

7. The delivery boy from Freitag's Delicatessen was the first act at the Halsey Theater's amateur night competition. What was his talent?

8. Who has had more years of schooling, Ralph or Alice?

9. How many cigars did Ed collect in the hospital waiting room while waiting for Alice's sister to give birth?

10. How did Ralph and Ed make back the money they lost with their glow-in-the-dark shoe polish scheme?

11. What product did Ralph and Ed plan on marketing under the name of "Kramnor's"?

12. Besides his silk handkerchiefs, what other item does Ed wash himself because he doesn't trust Trixie to wash it?

13. Where did Ralph buy the watch that was supposed to be given to the boss's daughter as a wedding present?

14. What was wrong with Ralph's bus that caused him to have an accident and break his leg?

15. Ralph thinks Alice is trying to kill him by putting poison in his tomato juice. What did Alice really put in the juice?

16. When Ralph and Ed ended up in court over a television set, which one of them was the plaintiff in the case?

17. In which episode do we see Ralph kiss Ed on the cheek?

18. What did Trixie throw at Ed that caused him to leave home and never want to return?

19. How old was the baby that Ralph found on his bus?

20. In "Battle of the Sexes," what song do Ralph and Ed sing while cleaning up the kitchen?

Last But Not Least

1. A. The Honeymooners go to Fred's Landing
   B. The Honeymooners go on a Racoon fishing trip
   C. The Honeymooners go to the Statler Hotel

2. A. The Racoons' convention is in New York City
   B. The Racoons' convention is in Minneapolis
   C. The Racoons' convention is in Chicago

3. A. Ralph buys an iron
   B. Ralph buys a vacuum cleaner
   C. Ralph buys a two-family house

4. A. Ralph and Ed buy a hotel
   B. Ralph and Ed buy a hot dog stand
   C. Ralph and Ed buy a summer cottage

5. A. Ralph Kramden meets Art Carney
   B. Ed Norton meets Jackie Gleason
   C. Ralph and Ed see Audrey Meadows

6. A. Rudy the Repairman stops by the Kramden apartment
   B. Joe the Bartender stops by the Kramden apartment
   C. Fenwick Babbitt stops by the Kramden apartment

7. A. Ed is wearing Trixie's dress
   B. Ed is dressed as Clara Bow
   C. Ed is dressed as Pierre Francois de la Brioski

8. A. Alice's sister Agnes gets married
   B. Alice's sister Sally gets married
   C. Alice's aunt Ethel gets married

9. A. Ralph breaks his leg in a bus accident
   B. Ralph hurts his back while bowling
   C. Ralph has a toothache

10. A. The Kramdens are on a quiz show
    B. The Kramdens are on *Beat the Clock*
    C. Ralph is on *The $99,000 Answer*

11. A. Ed dances with Frances Langford
    B. Ed dances with Harriett Muller
    C. Ed dances with a bowl of plaster

12. A. Ralph dances the Hucklebuck
    B. Ralph dances with Joe Malone's fiancée
    C. Ralph dances with Harriett Muller

13. A. Ed plays a harmonica
    B. Ed plays a coronet
    C. Ed plays a piano

14. A. Ralph finds a baby on the bus
    B. Ralph finds a suitcase on the bus
    C. Joe Cassidy finds $1,000.00 on the bus

The Honeymooners Episode Log

Included in the following episode guide are the earlier, extremely rare Honeymooners skits that were done as part of Gleason's *Cavalcade of Stars* (though they are not included in the quizzes). Also, attentive readers will notice that many of the episode names were repeated, beginning in the 1960s. The reason for this is that in the show's later incarnations, Jackie Gleason revisited old episodes, updating them with the new characters and actors because he felt the sketches could have a second life in color.

EPISODE NUMBER	EPISODE TITLE	ORIGINAL AIR DATE
	Cavalcade of Stars (1950–1952)	
1.	Bread	10/5/51
2.	Razor Blades	10/12/51
3.	New Television Set	11/2/51
4.	Ralph Threatens to Leave	11/16/51
5.	Ring Salesman	12/7/51
6.	Quiz Show	12/14/51
7.	Honeymooners Christmas Show 1951	12/21/51
	The Jackie Gleason Show (1952–1955)	
8.	Bowling	9/20/52
9.	The Turkey	9/27/52
10.	Lost Baby	10/11/52
11.	Quiz Show	10/18/52
12.	Masquerade	10/25/52
13.	The Cold	11/1/52
14.	Pickles	11/8/52
15.	The Jar of Jellybeans	11/22/52
16.	Missing Pants	12/6/52
17.	Six Months to Live	12/13/52
18.	Honeymooners Christmas Show 1952	12/20/52
19.	Glow Worm Cleansing Powder	1/3/53
20.	Alice Plays Cupid	1/17/53
21.	Suspense	1/24/53
22.	Lost Job	1/31/53
23.	Anniversary Gift	2/21/53
24.	Income Tax Time	3/7/53
25.	Alice's Aunt Ethel	3/14/53
26.	What's Her Name Again?	3/21/53
27.	Lunchbox	3/28/53
28.	Easter Hats	4/4/53
29.	Hot Tips	4/11/53
30.	Norton Moves In	4/18/53
31.	Ralph's Diet	4/25/53
32.	Dinner Guests	5/2/53
33.	Manager of the Baseball Team	5/9/53
34.	Alice's Birthday	5/16/53
35.	Dorsey Brothers Show	5/23/53
36.	The Prowler	6/6/53
37.	Guest Speaker	6/13/53
38.	Vacation at Fred's Landing	6/27/53

The Honeymooners (1955–1956)

The Jackie Gleason Show (1956–1957)

Jackie Gleason and His American Scene Magazine (1962–1966)

The Jackie Gleason Show "The Color Honeymooners" (1966–1970)

Answer Key

Episode Warm-up

1. R
2. N
3. K
4. A
5. I
6. D
7. G
8. H
9. P
10. F
11. O
12. C
13. E
14. Q
15. B
16. M
17. S
18. T
19. L
20. J

Theme Song Stumper

1. heavenly
   above
   heart
   desire
   greatest
   scheme
   charms
   me
   recall
   poems
   heart
   love
   greatest
   me
   greater
   heart
   love
2. B
3. A
4. Songsmiths, Inc.

Just This Once

1. Happy Larry Barnaby (11)
2. Dynamite Moran (54)
3. Mr. Lewis (56)
4. Dr. Durgom (64)
5. Nurse Campbell (64)
6. Charlotte Stattleman (77)
7. Herman Gruber (77)
8. Toots Mondello (88)
9. Adele Paterson (136)

First Things First

1. A (10)
2. C (72)
3. C (33)
4. B (33)
5. A (11)
6. A (52)
7. B (65)
8. B (43)
9. C (48)
10. A (138)
11. B (41)
12. B (101)

"Lost Episodes" ID

1. Q
2. J
3. A
4. K
5. I
6. C
7. P
8. H
9. L
10. M
11. O
12. F
13. R
14. E
15. G
16. T
17. N
18. S
19. D
20. B

Don't I Know You?

1. Joe the Bartender (48)
2. The Poor Soul (48)
3. Rudy the Repairman (48)
4. Reggie Van Gleason III (48)
5. Fenwick Babbitt (48)
6. Jackie Gleason (cameo) (138)

Korpulent Kramden

1. small; tall; hall; wall; wall (129)
2. any other elephant (108)
3. lucky if you can walk (106)
4. manhole; city; fit through (125)
5. round; square (110)
6. round one (87)
7. big fat tub (76)
8. tough; farmers (104)
9. pound; millionaire (95)
10. circus; bathing; elephant (84)

Family Matters

1. Elizabeth Wharton
2. C
3. A
4. D
5. Lillywhite (74)
6. C

7. B
8. Syracuse, New York
9. B
10. A. Galway, Ireland; B. Astoria; C. Pittsburgh; D. Buffalo; E. Dayton

Facts and Figures

1. B
2. C
3. B
4. A
5. Ray Bloch
6. Sammy Spear
7. "People to People"
8. D
9. C
10. A
11. "What's Her Name?" (7 minutes, 2 seconds)
12. "A Weighty Problem" (48 minutes, 9 seconds)

Name that Character I

1. Tommy Manicotti (119)
2. Mr. Johnson-landlord (128)
3. Bill Davis (129)
4. Carlos Sanchez (113)
5. Mr. Garrity, a.k.a. McGarrity (108)
6. Mrs. Simpson (107)
7. Teddy Oberman (98)
8. Millie Davis (129)
9. Henry Becker (80)

Q&A

1. I don't care if you burn (123)
2. There's a screw loose (84)
3. It was a dark, dark day (125)
4. Kiss me, Ralph (62)
5. a monkey only has one (61)
6. human being (107)
7. for two more (83)
8. sewing your pants
9. Too long
   Don't make me laugh
   is a bum (101)
10. You'll step on your finger (74)

Who Said That?

1. Ed; Trixie (97)
2. Alice; Ralph; Alice (136)
3. Ralph; Alice (94)
4. Ed; Ralph (101)
5. Mr. Marshall; Mr. Tebbets; Mr. Peck (111)
6. Jackie Gleason (138)
7. Ralph; Thelma the Maid (94)
8. Freddie Muller (134)
9. Wallace (110)
10. Mr. Faversham; Ed (121)

Out of Place

1. "The Adoption"; episodes in which Ralph thinks Alice is pregnant
2. Andre of the Plaza; great male chefs, according to Ed (117)
3. "The Lawsuit"; episodes that were repeated in the 1950s
4. Stanley Diamond; Alice's ex-boyfriends
5. Blitzen; the only three reindeer Ralph can name—sort of (47)
6. Tom Sawyer; books on the Winters' bookshelf (56)
7. Violet; the three cans of paint that Ed brought down to Ralph (56)
8. Eggplant purple; names that Alice gave to billiard balls (74)
9. Basil Fomeen; bands from the Sons of Italy Hall that Ralph mentions (110)
10. Fogarty boy; players on Ed's stickball team who got the measles (105)
11. "Mama Loves Mambo"; episodes in which Trixie does not appear
12. Freddy Muller; characters played by Frank Marth

Mug Shots

1. Gus Steinhart: Fraud (58)
2. Danny and Bibbo: Murder/Bank Robbery (119)
3. Marty: Racketeering (55)
4. Bullets Durgom: Murder/Jailbreak (46)
5. Boss and Ziggy: Counterfeiting (92)
6. Rocky and Lefty: Bookmaking (47)
7. Joe: Armed Robbery (80)
8. Barney Hackett: Racketeering (Boss) (55)

Bensonhurst's Most Wanted

1. C
2. B
3. D
4. B
5. A
6. C
7. A
8. D
9. B
10. A

Complete the Quote

1. fortune; fortune; going broke (97)
2. cat (126)
3. feeding; zoo (106)
4. sterile (95)
5. tunnel of love (136)
6. kleptomaniac (71)
7. starve (45)
8. armature; combustion; flow (101)
9. garbage man; dinner (37)
10. space; Captain Video (91)

First Honeymoon

1. D
2. B
3. C

4. a 1957 four-door sedan deluxe (135)
5. "Guest Speaker"
6. "Vacation at Fred's Landing"
7. D (74)
8. A (92)
9. "TV or Not TV" (91)
10. C (80)
11. a trick camera
12. Joe

At the Movies

1. A. "Champagne and Caviar"
   B. "What's Her Name Again?"
   C. "Letter to the Boss"
   D. "Double Anniversary"
   E. "Kramden vs. Norton"
   F. "The Love Letter"
   G. "The Babysitter"
2. Burning Lips
3. D
4. Ralph's boss is coming to dinner.
5. The Bowery Boys in Baghdad
6. The Halsey Theater; Love Conquers All
7. B
8. Ed Norton
9. to baby-sit Harvey Wahlstetter Jr.
10. the Halsey Theater

Who's Who

1) Pert Kelton
2) Five
3) Pert Kelton, Gingr Jones (filling in for Kelton), Audrey Meadows, Sue Anne Langdon, Sheila MacRae
4) Four
5) Elaine Stritch, Joyce Randolph, Patricia Wilson, Jane Kean
6) Audrey Meadows
7) Herbert John Gleason
8) Arthur William Matthew Carney

Money Matters

1) 93 cents (118)
2) $200.00 (61)
3) A (97)
4) A
5) C
6) B (99)
7) C (104)
8) $600.00 (41)
9) C
10) B (107)

Police Blotter

1. A
2. C
3. D
4. B
5. B
6. A
7. C
8. B (30)
9. C (48)
10. D

First Name Basis

1. Whitey (48)
2. Harry (80)
3. Mike (77)
4. Ethel (77)
5. Dorothy (83)
6. Bruce (65)
7. Wallace (110)
8. Thelma (94)
9. Zelda (160)
10. Andre (115)
11. Brigid (148)
12. Emily (93)
13. Frederick (121)
14. Hamilton (121)
15. Rachel (121)
16. Harvey (127)
17. George (127)
18. Jose (108)
19. Luigi (146)
20. Angelo (146)
21. Marty (92)
22. Frank (107)

23. Charlie (124)

24. Bucky (65)

25. Felix (72)

26. Durgom (138)

27. Martin (20)

28. Henrietta (21)

Norton in Disguise

1. Uncle Sam; "Forgot to Register"

2. A merry Mouseketeer; "My Fair Landlord"

3. A mind-reading swami; "Songs and Witty Sayings"

4. Clara Bow; "Halloween Party"

5. Santa's elf; "Santa Claus and the Bookies"

6. A bellboy; "The Brother-in-Law"

7. Ray Bloch; "Songs and Witty Sayings"

8. Pierre Francois de la Brioski; "Petticoat Jungle"

9. Stan Laurel; "Songs and Witty Sayings"

Triple Elimination

1. "Ralph Kramden, Inc.," "The Worry Wart," "Finders Keepers"

2. "Quiz Show," "Income Tax Time," "Dinner Guests"

3. "Suspense," "Better Living Through TV," "Oh My Aching Back"

4. "The Safety Award," "Alice and the Blonde," "Catch a Star"

5. "Norton Moves In," "Halloween Party," "Honeymooners Christmas Show 1953"

6. "A Matter of Life and Death," "The Deciding Vote," "The Babysitter"

7. "The Great Jewel Robbery," "One Big Happy Family," "Songs and Witty Sayings"

8. "The Cold"

Don't Touch Me, I'm Sterile...

1. A. Obstetrician (133)

   B. A.k.a. "The Mad Butcher of Bensonhurst" (64)

   C. Bus company physician (49)

   D. Diagnosed Ralph and Ed with the measles (105)

   E. Treated Ed after a manhole cover fell on his head (98)

   F. Took blood from Ralph for a transfusion (98)

   G. Veterinarian (95)

   H. The only doctor who can cure arterial monochromia (95)

2. Pentothal (96)

3. The psychiatrist diagnoses that Norton irritates Ralph, and that Ralph must stop hanging around with his neighbor in order to get better. (78)

4. Michael Case, a.k.a. "The Great Fatchoomara" (76)

5. Her sacroiliac was acting up. (47)

Game Show Showdown

1. D

2. Popular Songs

3. Herb Norris (108)

4. A

5. eight

6. C

7. Bud Collyer (70)

8. C (70)

9. cup; whipped cream; net; mouth (70)

10. B (70)

11. "Act in haste, and repent at leisure." (70)

12. $300.00 in cash, two baby carriages, and a Sylvania TV set (70)

13. a year's supply of Krinkly Krax breakfast cereal (11)

14. "The breakfast food that makes you wish it was lunchtime." (11)

15. Mrs. Gibson (11)

16. Happy Larry Barnaby (11)

17. California (11)

18. Marcaroni (11)

We're in Business

1. A. Gym (127)

   B. Employment agency (94)

   C. Department store (103)

   D. Motel (63)

   E. Drugstore (77)

   F. Sporting goods store (136)

   G. Bar and grill (132)

   H. Pizzeria (118)

   I. Iron company (125)

   J. Gasoline station (128)

   K. Bowling alley (135)

   L. Hotel (49)

   M. Candy store (137)

2. A. Where Ralph bought a secondhand vacuum (101)

   B. Redecorating the Kramdens' apartment free (115)

   C. Where Alice and Trixie bought the same dress (124)

   D. Owned by Irving Shapiro (23)

   E. Alice likes their lychee nuts (129)

   F. Ralph rented a tuxedo from here (112)

   G. The best place to get lasagna (48)

   H. The best place to get potato salad (48)

   I. The place where Ralph got a hot tip on a horse (61)

Handy Housewife Helper

1. B

2. C

3. about one minute (if they knocked on the Kramdens' door first)

4. D

5. Ed is the Chef of the Past; Ralph is the Chef of the Future

6. C

7. A

8. C, A, B

9. in the Bronx

10. D

Caller ID

1. A. BEnsonhurst 6-0098 (129)

   B. BEnsonhurst 6-0099 (77)

   C. EVergreen 4-2598 (77)

   D. MELrose-5099 (61)

   E. BEnsonhurst 5-6698 (97)

   F. BEnsonhurst 0-7741 (107)

   G. BEnsonhurst 0-7740 (107)

2. "The Babysitter"; "Funny Money"

3. B (76)

4. the Brooklyn recruiting office of the French Foreign Legion

5. A

Twenty-three Skidoo

1. Alice; Aunt

2. Guest

3. Good Night Sweet

4. Party; Boss

5. Alice

6. Kramden; Norton

7. Anniversary

8. Letter

9. Ralph; Sweet

10. Dog; Life

11. Christmas

12. Alice

13. Party

14. Anniversary

15. Letter; Boss

16. Ralph

17. Life

18. Two Family

19. Ralph Kramden

20. Night; Christmas

21. Lost

22. Hot Dog

23. Family

24. Young Man

25. Hot

26. Lost

27. Man

28. Good; Aunt

29. Matter; Life

30. Two

31. Young

32. Matter

33. Norton

34. Man

Number Cruncher

1. B (64)

2. D (40)

3. D (135)

4. A (47)

5. C (95)

6. Cigar Box: 6; Happy Feet: 4 (61)

7. B (61)

8. 247

9. 25: as a word 16 times, as a numeral 9 times (108)

10. A: 4 and 11; B: 11 and 13; C: 5 and 7 (48)

11. "treats wife like workhorse" (116)

12. "argues too much" (116)

Family Album

1. Sally Gibson-Diamond; Alice's sister (65)

2. Mrs. Kramden; Ralph's mother (100)

3. Leo; Alice's uncle (103)

4. George; Alice's uncle (42)

5. Agnes Gibson-Saxon; Alice's sister (112)

6. Stanley Saxon; Brother-in-law (112)

7. Stanley Diamond; Brother-in-law (65)

8. Mrs. Gibson; Alice's mother (80)

9. Frank Gibson; Alice's brother (71)

"Classic 39" ID

1. "Oh My Aching Back"

2. "The Worry Wart"

3. "Dial J For Janitor"

4. "The Babysitter"

5. "A Man's Pride"

6. "Young Man with a Horn"

7. "Head of the House"

8. "Trapped"

9. "The Safety Award"

10. "Mind Your Own Business"

11. "Ralph Kramden, Inc."

12. "Here Comes the Bride"

13. "A Matter of Record"

14. "TV or Not TV"

15. "Funny Money"

16. "The Golfer"

17. "Better Living Through TV"

18. "A Woman's Work Is Never Done"

19. "Mama Loves Mambo"

20. "Unconventional Behavior"

21. "Please Leave the Premises"

22. "Young at Heart"

23. "Alice and the Blonde"

24. "A Matter of Life and Death"

25. "The Sleepwalker"

26. "Pal o' Mine"

27. "The Deciding Vote"

28. "Hello, Mom"

29. "The $99,000 Answer"

30. "'Twas the Night Before Christmas"

31. "Something Fishy"

32. "On Stage"

33. "The Bensonhurst Bomber"

34. "Opportunity Knocks But"

35. "The Loudspeaker"

36. "Pardon My Glove"

37. "A Dog's Life"

38. "Brother Ralph"

39. "The Man from Space"

"Letter to the Boss"

1. Marshall; bum; lowlife; membership; human; nine; safely; meanest; world; bum; Respectfully; etcetera etcetera

2. Because he hangs his left arm out of the bus window.

3. thirty-six undershirt sleeves

4. C

5. He says they are writing a play about a mailbox.
6. A
7. three; 1,000.00
8. B

Petrie Puzzler

1. Stanton (131)
2. Muller (134)
3. George (138)
4. priest (24)
5. Williams (37)
6. lawyer (52)
7. Philbin (54)
8. Nick (55)
9. cop (56)
10. Bob (64)
11. Jerry (70)
12. surveyor (71)
13. Case (76)
14. psychiatrist (78)
15. Callahan (80)
16. Joe (81)
17. doctor (82)
18. emcee (88)
19. Diamond (65)
20. desk clerk (138)
21. Thomas (52)
22. mobster (55)
23. reporter (64)
24. Petrie (71)
25. waiter (81)
26. Rocky (47)
27. Danny (119)

Family Gossip

1. false; it was his uncle Herman (54)
2. true (13)
3. true (43)
4. false; he is a notary public
5. true
6. false; it was his parents' fiftieth anniversary (56)
7. false; Agnes is married to Stanley Saxon (112)
8. true (106)

9. true (65)
10. true (58)
11. false; she is Alice's cousin (77)
12. true (70)
13. false; she did not attend (61)
14. false; it was her brother Frank (71)
15. true (135)
16. false; it was Zeppo Marx (138)
17. true (71)
18. false; it's Alice's brother (137)
19. true (135)
20. true (107)

Best Friends

1. 142 years old (139)
2. Ed used a lighter to read the thermometer.
3. wires under the hood of a car; a toaster
4. C (109)
5. "Santa Claus and the Bookies"
6. "The Deciding Vote"
7. grape juice (117)
8. B (74)
9. A (125)
10. He sprained his ankle. (40)
11. D
12. "Ralph Kramden, Inc."
13. false; Ralph's mother was sick and Ed borrowed the car (40)
14. true (136)
15. Eduardo (113)

Stage Fright

1. It had to be refrigerated. (64)
2. C (64)
3. bus driver; brain surgeon; goody (64)
4. A (64)
5. B (64)
6. talking; nervous; Norton (97)
7. James Cagney (121)
8. Herbert J. Whiteside (121)
9. D (121)

10. "Our Friends the Animals" (88)
11. take a trip to Florida (88)
12. a hula song and dance (88)
13. custard pie; whipped cream blueberry pie (88)
14. "I brive a dus...I dus a brive" (108)

Dimwit Ed

1. The guy lived for almost eight months. (95)
2. "I don't have to practice it, I know it." (95)
3. "b-u-t-e-y" (136)
4. Ile de France (129)
5. pack up and move to Florida (116)
6. poloponies (121)
7. a swami; algebra (88)
8. the 18th: "Tell them you were drunk." (118)
9. hold a dance (138)
10. plaster for the ceiling (55)

What's His Name?

1. Bill Zuckert
2. Ned Glass
3. Sid Raymond
4. Frank Marth
5. Eddie Hanley
6. Humphrey Davis
7. Boris Aplon
8. Dick Bernie
9. George Petrie
10. Charles Korvin
11. Ronnie Burns
12. Luis Van Rooten
13. John Griggs I
14. Alexander Clark I
15. Les Damon

The Gotham Bus Company

1. 225 River Street (45)
2. A: Claims Adjuster; B: Payroll; C: Secretary; D: Traffic Manager; E: President; F: Dispatcher; G: Bus Driver; H: Doctor; I: Vice President

3. 2368 (162)
4. Six (61)
5. No. 802 (84) and No. 247 (137)
6. "A Dog's Life" (111)

Mother-in-Law

1. B (105)
2. D (105)
3. go to Florida with Mr. Gibson (92)
4. the Statler Hotel to see the Dorsey Brothers (49)
5. Alice's birthday (80)
6. A (105)
7. Ralph's mother (100)
8. Alice's uncle Leo (106)
9. B
10. criticized; misunderstood; defenseless (100)

Facts about Norton

1. B (97)
2. A (118)
3. B (121)
4. D (56)
5. C (109)
6. "Swanee River" (105)
7. "What is your name?"; he was too nervous (11)
8. A: "Funny Money"; B: "The Next Champ"; C: "Quiz Show"; D: "Lost Job"
9. D (125)
10. C (117)

Street Smarts

1. B (107)
2. C (107)
3. A
4. B (55)
5. D (47)
6. A (137)
7. C
8. B (23)
9. A (40)
10. B (104)

Rendezvous

1. A. a week from Friday at 6:00 p.m.; Laurel Gardens (54)
   B. the 21st of the month at 10:00 a.m.; IRS office (118)
   C. 9:30 p.m.; Colonnade Room (129)
   D. 12:30 p.m.; City Hall (124)
   E. Friday at 8:00 p.m.; Kelsey's Gym (127)
   F. 6:00 p.m.; Montgomery Street (47)
2. B (109)
3. C (44)
4. A (77)
5. B (129)
6. C (47)

One of These Days, Alice...

1. February 8 (83)
2. Gibson
3. Troop 35, Red-wing Patrol (79)
4. B
5. "Suspense"(10) and "On Stage" (121)
6. B (A, 94) (C, 107) (D, 22)
7. Blue (82)
8. To stick to her diet, to keep within her budget, and to not fight with Ralph anymore
9. P.S. 73 (136)
10. "Expectant Fathers" (133)

Show Me the Money

1. B (54)
2. A (54)
3. B (13)
4. D (15)
5. B (49)
6. A. Ralph: $16.00; B. Alice: $7.00; C. Bill: $12.00; D. Millie: $9.00 (129)
7. C (76)
8. C (76)
9. D (51)
10. A (118)

Howdy, Neighbor

1. A. Radiator doesn't work
   B. Venetian blinds are broken
   C. Bathtub needs fixing
   D. Bathroom sink needs fixing
   E. Something is missing out of her icebox
   F. "Eureka, my garbage can is full"
   G. Doesn't have any water (128)
2. A (113)
3. D
4. the Nortons (74)
5. B
6. A
7. C (118)
8. C
9. D (48)
10. B

Moving Out

1. A (139)
2. invites Ralph
3. brown
4. misty gray (139)
5. green (139)
6. Mr. and Mrs. George Winters
7. Albany, N.Y. (56)
8. sublet their old apartment (56)
9. Flushing, Queens
10. a bar of soap
11. $90.00 a month
12. C
13. Captain Video and His Video Rangers
14. Paradise Acres

Last Name Scramble

1. Tasselman (83)
2. Grime (84)
3. Olsen (139)
4. Simpson (107)
5. Johnson (128)
6. Wiggams (128)
7. Schwartz (128)
8. Martin (124)
9. Parker (108)
10. O'Donnell (109)

11. Bascom (109)
12. Carson (109)
13. Bradley (109)
14. Reynolds (94)
15. Gersch (95)
16. Morris (61)
17. Hartman (61)
18. Prescott (117)
19. Taylor (54)
20. Fensterblau (117)

Wall of Fame

1. Frances Langford; "Honeymooners Christmas Show 1953"
2. Jimmy Dorsey; "New Year's Eve Party with the Dorseys"
3. Ray Bloch; "Catch a Star"
4. Tommy Dorsey; "New Year's Eve Party with the Dorseys"
5. Bud Collyer; "Teamwork Beat the Clock"

Fact or Fiction

1. fact
2. fact
3. fiction
4. fiction; it is in Bushwick, Brooklyn
5. fact
6. fiction
7. fact
8. fact
9. fiction; Lake Pokamoonshine is in New York
10. fact; George and Patti Petrie were really married to each other
11. fiction
12. fiction; the Park Sheraton Hotel was used only for rehearsals

Seeing Double

1. A and C
2. B and C
3. B and D
4. D
5. A and D
6. B and C
7. C and D
8. A and B
9. B and D
10. B and C

Matchmaker

1. Dorothy (83)
2. Charlotte (77)
3. Gladys (49)
4. Helen (124)
5. Henrietta (21)
6. Rita (126)
7. Millie (129)
8. Ethel (62)
9. Agnes (112)
10. Sally (65)
11. Angelina (113)
12. Helen (107)
13. Gladys (56)
14. Elizabeth
15. Alice
16. Thelma
17. Sarah (106)
18. Helen (70)
19. Harriet (33)

Scenic Recall

1. "The Next Champ"
2. "The Love Letter"
3. "Ralph's Sweet Tooth"
4. "The Little Man Who Wasn't There"
5. "New Year's Eve Party with the Dorseys"
6. "This Is Your Life"
7. "Songs and Witty Sayings"
8. "Kramden vs. Norton"
9. "Teamwork Beat the Clock"
10. "The Great Jewel Robbery"
11. "Cupid"
12. "Alice and the Blonde"
13. "Vacation at Fred's Landing"
14. "Letter to the Boss"
15. "The Man in the Blue Suit"
16. "Battle of the Sexes"
17. "The Sleepwalker"
18. "Stars over Flatbush"
19. "Santa Claus and the Bookies"
20. "Young at Heart"
21. "Game Called on Account of Marriage"
22. "The Brother-in-Law"
23. "Catch a Star"
24. "Finders Keepers"
25. "The Babysitter"

'Tis the Season

1. A: Ed to Ralph; B: Ralph to Ed; C: Uncle Leo to Ralph and Alice; D: Mrs. Gibson to Ralph; E: Alice to Ralph; F: Mrs. Stevens to Alice; G: Alice to Mrs. Stevens
2. Ralph Kramden, Fenwick Babbitt, Joe the bartender, the Poor Soul, Rudy the repairman, Reggie Van Gleason III
3. Alice and Trixie both got a Napoleon-shaped juice extractor
4. holiday playboy

Who Am I?

1. Trixie's mother (54)
2. Jack Philbin (54)
3. Tino Barzi (49)
4. Herbert Johnson (49)
5. Doreen Lewis (135)
6. Ralphina Kramden (82)
7. Mamie Murphy (48)
8. Shorty (78)
9. Ed Norton (70)
10. Arline Judge (26)
11. Henry Becker (70)
12. Evelyn Fensterblau (77)
13. Charlotte Stattleman (77)
14. Cora Brenstetter (81)
15. Knuckles Grogan (47)
16. Larry Spencer (65)
17. Ray Bloch (71)
18. Tommy and Jimmy Dorsey (49)
19. Art Carney (138)
20. Herb Armstrong (54)

The Kramdens

1. The Hotel New Yorker
2. B
3. Ralphina (82)
4. A (105)
5. A (77)
6. With Alice's parents, for four years
7. C (91)
8. BEnsonhurst 0-7741 (107)
9. Bunny (105)
10. Buttercup (105)

The Golfer

1. Mr. Harper
2. Silver Oaks
3. Saturday, changed to Sunday
4. 10:00 A.M.
5. "Step up, plant your feet firmly, and address the ball."
6. He says, "Hello, ball."
7. A
8. C

Name that Character II

1. August Gunther (116)
2. Rita Wedemeyer (126)
3. Harvey Wahlstetter Jr. (107)
4. Mr. Bartfeld (107)
5. Mrs. Gunther (116)
6. Burt Wedemeyer (126)
7. Mr. Bartfeld-candy store owner (137)
8. Helen Wahlstetter (107)
9. Angelina Manicotti (113)

Stand In for Murder

1. B
2. C
3. an insurance company
4. Prudential Insurance
5. D
6. A
7. C
8. true; the ending of this episode was cut off because it ran overtime on live television

9. D
10. B

What Did You Call Me?

1. Ed
2. Trixie
3. Alice
4. Ed
5. Alice
6. Rita Wedemeyer
7. Alice
8. Wallace
9. Alice
10. Burt Wedemeyer
11. Judy Connors
12. Ralph
13. Alice
14. Alice
15. Ralph
16. Ralph
17. Alice
18. Ed
19. Alice
20. Ralph
21. Ed
22. Ralph
23. Ralph
24. Alice
25. Alice
26. Trixie

What's Her Name?

1. Ethel Owen
2. Patti Pope Petrie
3. Anne Seymour
4. Zamah Cunningham
5. Freda Rosen
6. Gingr Jones
7. Betty Garde
8. Abby Lewis

Behind the Scenes

1. Jack Philbin
2. Jack Hurdle
3. Stanley Poss
4. Frank Satenstein
5. Marvin Marx

6. Walter Stone
7. Herbert Finn
8. A.J. Russell
9. Leonard Stern
10. Sydney Zelinka
11. Jack Lescoulie
12. Leonard Anderson

Food for Thought

1. E (50)
2. C (54)
3. D (133)
4. K (28)
5. I (49)
6. O (106)
7. Q (117)
8. H (13)
9. L (139)
10. M (54)
11. P (54)
12. R (23)
13. F (123)
14. B (28)
15. N (55)
16. A (21)
17. G (21)
18. J (50)

The Gift-Giver's Guide

1. broom (25)
2. belt (136)
3. Gimbel's (49)
4. candy rabbit (23)
5. necktie (56)
6. newspaper (49)
7. muffler (49)
8. reducing (46)
9. cigar (128)
10. coronet (116)
11. tiepin (76)
12. convertible (55)
13. rhinestone (48)
14. African (48)
15. Rangoon (48)
16. mahogany (48)
17. gloves (48)
18. watch (80)

19. pot holders (80)
20. decoder (80)
21. dress (80)
22. scarf (74)

In the Hotel Business

1. "The Brother-in-Law"
2. Frank
3. He was a bellhop.
4. He drinks it from the saucer.
5. Crestwood Hotel
6. $500.00
7. New Jersey
8. A. manager
   B. chef
   C. bellhop
   D. chambermaid
9. No. 3
10. George Petrie
11. a pack of cigarettes
12. GENIUS AT WORK
13. B
14. A: 5; B: 7; C: 2; D: 6; E: 1;
    F: 4; G: 3

Name that Character III

1. Judge Lawrence Norton Hurdle
   (124)
2. Joe Fensterblau (117)
3. Frederick Carson (109)
4. Herb Norris (108)
5. Miss Lawrence (82)
6. Harvey (127)
7. Mr. Faversham (121)
8. Thelma the Maid (94)
9. George (127)

What Did I Borrow?

1. shoe polish
2. beaded handbag
3. three oranges (103)
4. handkerchief
5. Freddie Muller (124)
6. monkey wrench
7. headache powder
8. mercurochrome
9. black dress

10. bowling shoes; fishing pole
11. Carlos Sanchez (113)
12. black thread
13. raw carrot
14. hairpin

A Night at the Lodge

1. west; east; beast; courage;
   chips; break; brother; tails;
   spirit; hearts; trees; seven
   seas; brothers; noble (72)
2. Mr. Alfredo (72)
3. $100.00 (72)
4. Hurricanes (106)
5. C (76)
6. A (61)
7. Stanley Saxon (112)
8. Acme Finance Company (121)
9. E PLURIBUS RACOON (76)
10. D (138)

Classic, Lost, or Late Model?

1. Lost Episode (44)
2. Lost Episode (76)
3. Classic 39 (123)
4. Late Model (170)
5. Classic 39 (125)
6. Late Model (189)
7. Classic 39 (114)
8. Lost Episode (24)
9. Lost Episode (67)
10. Late Model (182)
11. Classic 39 (118)
12. Classic 39 (120)
13. Late Model (185)
14. Lost Episode (134)
15. Lost Episode (75)
16. Classic 39 (122)
17. Lost Episode (48)
18. Late Model (180)
19. Lost Episode (87)
20. Lost Episode (37)

Denizens of the Deep

1. B (65)
2. A (74)
3. A (88)

4. D (136)
5. C (136)
6. B
7. A (74)
8. B (125)
9. paradise (115)
10. mud; eye (117)
11. holes (93)
12. Time; tide (109)

Get the Facts Straight

1. C (A: 69; B: 83)
2. A (B: 83; C: 69)
3. C (A: 55; B 93)
4. B (A: 24; C: 50, D: 136)
5. A (B: 24; C: 36, D: 21)
6. D (A: 78; B: 74, C: 44)
7. B (A: 47; C: 133)
8. D (A: 124; B: 56; C: 41)

The Icebox, the Sink, and the Bureau

1. C (100)
2. A (100)
3. D
4. B (119)
5. B
6. the icebox door, the sink's
   faucet, and the knobs from
   the bureau (104)
7. C (42)
8. Liberace (91)
9. a cigarette
10. D

The Flab Four

RALPH

1. $45.00 and the bus (61)
2. Jackie Gleason (44)
3. a pinball machine (104)
4. baseball; basketball; jockey (44)
5. true (13)

ALICE

1. She took a commercial course
   in school. (99)
2. antidisestablishmentarianism
   (108)

3. tuna salad (113)

4. the top ring off a pickle barrel (43)

5. Jimmy Dorsey (49)

ED

1. Colonel Winthrop (62)

2. the Racoons' old-clothes drive (120)

3. pressure in the brain (128)

4. apples (133)

5. his wedding ring (56)

TRIXIE

1. Ajax (44)

2. a cookbook (136)

3. Frances Langford (48)

4. "Better Living Through TV"

5. her sister's

Name that Character IV

1. Richard Puder (118)

2. Mr. Monahan (129)

3. Freddie Muller (134)

4. Dr. Folsom (105)

5. Mr. Mitchell (58)

6. Tony Amico (99)

7. Dr. Agres (40)

8. Mr. Marshall (49)

9. Alice Kramden

Anniversary Quiz

1. B (130)

2. C (130)

3. B

4. A

5. D

6. C

7. B

8. A (B-24, 193; C-130; D-14)

9. A (77)

10. C

Tax Day

1. 23 Mockingbird Lane (84)

2. C (24)

3. B (118)

4. He forgot to sign his tax returns. (118)

5. He gives it to a priest as a donation for the poor. (24)

6. Three dollars he found floating in the sewer (118)

7. A (118)

Norton, Come on Down...

1. January 12 (74)

2. U.S. Navy (54)

3. Lillywhite (74)

4. 86 (136)

5. The Cougars (105)

6. Lulu (96)

7. 137

8. B

9. Walt Disney

10. D

The NYC Dept. of Subterranean Sanitation

1. "The city sewers can't be used for personal pleasure."

2. Himrod Street (98)

3. Bushwick Hospital, Room 317 (98)

4. Jim McKeever, aka Ol' Muck n' Mire (98)

5. Foreman of the 42nd Street outlet to the East River

6. tides, life, current, back, float (124)

All About Pets

1. A (109)

2. In the tunnel of love in Coney Island (96)

3. Happy Hound (60)

4. A pregnant cat (194)

5. A collie named Ginger (95)

6. C (111)

7. 3 (111)

I Have a Big Mouth

1. C (21)

2. B (26)

3. Jackie Gleason (138)

4. Joe Munsey (101)

5. D (45)

6. the bus company (131)

7. He's an assistant plumber. (129)

8. selling irons door-to-door (125)

9. Harvey (127)

10. George; Pittsburgh (42)

11. Stanley and Agnes (112)

12. the Statler Hotel (49)

Boys' Night Out

1. B

2. Alice

3. Alice (74)

4. C (106)

5. C (119)

6. A

7. D (106)

8. Ed is winning, 19-2; a dime

9. Freddie Muller's

10. A (77)

Hey There Ralphie Boy!

1. B (134)

2. P.S. 73 (77)

3. Sixth grade (169)

4. The $99,000 Answer, Beat the Clock, Krinkly Krax quiz show

5. Choosy Chews Candy (64), the Handy Housewife Helper (97), Flakey Wakey cereal (148)

6. C (108) (119) (121)

7. 5 feet, 11 inches (85)

8. 18 inches (46)

9. B (46)

10. D (118)

11. Type A (98)

12. B (169)

13. 246 pounds

Election Day

1. Harper and Penrose (132)

2. Penrose (132)

3. Harper (132)

4. C (101)

5. Weaver and Morgan (67)
6. To spend the lodge's budget surplus on beer and soda (61)

Unconventional Behavior

1. Ralph: A, C, D, F, H; Ed: B, E, G
2. Minneapolis, Minnesota
3. 11:15 P.M.
4. Norfolk, Virginia
5. Five days
6. 3 (upper and lower)
7. B
8. 320 feet/second

Weight Watcher

1. He's underweight by four pounds.
2. D
3. C
4. B
5. C
6. A
7. D
8. C
9. a reducing machine
10. "A Weighty Problem"

Fred's Landing

1. Atlantic City
2. two weeks
3. the Royal Hawaiian Motel
4. D
5. The bridge was over a railroad track.
6. Jimmy Nolan
7. A
8. two days
9. Ralph
10. C
11. one
12. paradise; Watchung; Pokamoonshine

Name That Tune

1. "You're My Greatest Love"
2. "The Hucklebuck" (110)
3. "Claves for Mambo," by Tito Rodriguez (113)

4. "Swanee River" (108)
5. A: Cole Porter; B: Warren-Dubin; C: Johnny Mercer and Richard Whiting; D: Ernesto Dequista
6. Ernesto Dequista

"Classic 39" Classic Lines

1. D (99, 107, 110, 112, 115, 117, 121, 122, 126)
2. C (108, 110, 112, 114, 120, 126, 128)
3. A (125)
4. B (92, 108, 119, 128)
5. core a apple (97)

Read All About It

1. mental (64)
2. D (118)
3. A
4. B (13)
5. C (32)
6. A (27)
7. B
8. A (124)
9. C
10. B (117)

Show and Tell

1. Dorothy-Joe Malone's fiancée (83)
2. He can't sleep. (134)
3. the head of a mop (135)
4. a Zulu chief (43)
5. whipped cream (70)
6. He has a toothache. (64)
7. Agnes and Stanley's wedding (112)
8. a grocery store delivery boy (78)
9. whipped cream blueberry pie (88)

Honeymooners in Disguise

1. A bear (37)
2. A gorilla (151)
3. Pierre Francois de la Brioski (104)
4. Henry VIII (104)

5. A sailor (104)
6. A 12-year-old girl (104)
7. A: Ed; B: Trixie; C: Alice; D: Ralph
8. An elegant bum

All About Trixie

1. C (74)
2. November 30 (83)
3. True (88)
4. A
5. "Floogle Street" (88)
6. "Honeymooners Christmas Show 1953" (48)
7. False (but her mother does)
8. "Suspense" (21)
9. "Unconventional Behavior" (123)

Complete the Title

1. Champ
2. Boys; Girls
3. Easter
4. Boxtop
5. Better Living; TV
6. Songs; Witty
7. Cottage
8. Stars; Flatbush
9. Alice; Cupid
10. Money
11. Weighty
12. Game; Account; Marriage
13. Glove
14. Fishy
15. Landlord
16. Man; Blue Suit
17. Opportunity Knocks
18. Mama; Mambo
19. Men; Horse
20. Jewel Robbery
21. Good Night; Prince
22. Young; Horn
23. Aunt Ethel
24. Little Man; Wasn't
25. Tickets; Fight
26. Matter; Life; Death
27. Norton; In

28. Woman's Work; Done
29. Principle
30. Aching Back

Hare-Brained Schemes

1. gasoline
2. Goat
3. Plastic
4. Uranium field
5. Glow-in-the-dark (58)
6. boxer (54)
7. New Jersey (155)
8. No-cal (97)
9. Captain Kidd
10. Housewife (97)
11. Kranmars, Mystery (111)
12. hair (58)

The Trip to Europe

1. taste; fat little waist (143)
2. Paris, France (145)
3. Tony (146)
4. Ralph kills a rabbit; Ed kills an elephant. (151)
5. Dunellin, Ireland (147)
6. C (A: 149) (B: 148) (D: 150)
7. Miguel and Rosita (149)

All About the Racoons

1. A
2. B
3. D
4. Fingers, fingers, thumbs, thumbs
5. A, D
6. B, C, E
7. Brother Gavin's

Get Out!!!

1. Never
2. 21 (91, three times; 94; 100; 101; 102; 104; 105; 112; 113; 115, two times; 117; 118, two times; 119; 120; 122; 125; 129)
3. 2 (101, 113)
4. 1 (113)

5. Never
6. 1 (99)
7. 2 (113, two times)
8. 1 (98)
9. 2 (92, 105)
10. 1 (113)

Potluck Final Exam

1. gray
2. A
3. Rudy the Repairman (48)
4. true (48)
5. false; it was Ralph's brother Leo (88)
6. model-airplane building (78)
7. He played music using a bicycle air pump. (88)
8. Alice-eight years (11)
9. eight (70)
10. by polishing shoes (58)
11. a hair restorer (58)
12. his Howdy Doody T-shirt (80)
13. Steinhart's jewelry store (80)
14. The windshield wipers didn't work.
15. a vitamin (22)
16. Ralph (74)
17. "Peacemaker"
18. a bowl of soup (22)
19. two months (10)
20. "Raggmopp"

Last But Not Least

1. B (112)
2. B (123)
3. C (139)
4. A (71)
5. B (138)
6. A (48)
7. C (104)
8. A (110)
9. B (106)
10. C (108)
11. C (55)
12. A (110)
13. B (116)
14. A (137)

Photo Credits